BMW

Other Titles in the Crowood MotoClassics Series

BMW MOTORCYCLES

THE COMPLETE STORY

BRUCE PRESTON

The Crowood Press

First published in 1990 by
The Crowood Press Ltd
Ramsbury, Marlborough
Wiltshire SN8 2HR

Revised edition 1996

This impression 2002

British Library Cataloguing-in-Publication Data
A catalogue record for this book is available from the British Library.

ISBN 1 86126 005 9

Typeset by Phoenix Typesetting, Burley-in-Wharfedale, West Yorkshire

Printed and bound in Great Britain by Bookcraft, Midsomer Norton

Contents

Preface

It is a daunting task to sit down and attempt to write a history of BMW motorcycles. As time goes on, the early history, if not recorded soon after, becomes either lost or blurred. Many fine, and often unsung, authors have written books about BMW.

What qualifications do I bring to the task? Because I have owned BMW motorcycles for over thirty years I am sometimes described as an expert. I am not. I am an enthusiast, for motorcycles in general and BMWs in particular. I know a little about some of the models. Researching this book has once again shown me that there are a great many true experts in the world who *really* know about BMWs. It is the good fortune of those of us who write that few of them have the time or inclination to become authors. It is our even better fortune that many of them give their knowledge freely for others to share and make use of.

I hope that, with this book, the information and knowledge that I have gained will enable me to share my enthusiasm not only with other BMW buffs but with all who love motorcycles.

Acknowledgements

I would like to thank my good friends Bob Porecha, Alberto Criscolo and Charles Lock for so willingly sharing their considerable knowledge of BMW motorcycles. In particular, thanks should go to Joe Greenwood (who sadly died in December 1989) for allowing me to quote from his series, 'In Search of BMW', published in the *BMW Club Journal*. It remains one of the best BMW stories written.

Thanks to Peter Zollner, archivist at BMW in Munich, for the use of the considerable BMW library of photographs and to Franz Marek of Austria for allowing me to photograph his superb collection. Particular thanks to the National Motor Museum at Beaulieu for the use of archive material.

Were he still alive, there would be a special thank you to my old friend Keith Sanders. We joined the BMW Club on the same day in 1958 and it was his enthusiasm and knowledge that kept me on my toes all of these years. He succumbed to a stroke in 1987. I wish he was still here to continue to offer his good advice. A final thank you to all the many friends who over the years have made owning a BMW motorcycle special.

BMW: A BRIEF HISTORY

1913 Rapp-Motorenwerke established by Karl Rapp.

1915 OttoWerke formed.

1916 Rapp and Otto companies merge to form Bayerische Flugzeugwerke with Franz Josef Popp, Max Friz and Camillo Castiglioni as the principals.

1917 BFW renamed Bayerische Motoren Werke.

1919 BMW 1V aircraft reaches a world altitude record.

1921 First motorcycle engine, the M2B15, is produced. It is used in the Helios – and many other makes.

1922 Rudolf Schleicher makes the first-ever light alloy cylinder head, which is used on the R32.

1923 First BMW motorcycle, the R32, manufactured.

1924 The R37, the racing derivative of the R32, wins the first championship for BMW.

1925 The first single-cylinder machine, the R39, is made.

1926 A supercharged racing motorcycle is produced. BMW and Mercedes–Benz sign a contract agreeing that Mercedes would concentrate on cars and BMW would concentrate on aircraft and motorcycles whilst also making a small car.

1927 First of three consecutive wins in the Targa Florio.

1928 BMW buy Dixi-Werke and the first BMW-Dixi car produced, an Austin 7, is made under licence.

1929 A BMW motorcycle ridden by Ernst Henne using a super-charged 750cc engine breaks the absolute world motorcycle record. The pressed steel 'star' frame is introduced. First BMW car produced.

1930 BMW temporarily retire from motor-cycle racing.

1935 The first hydraulically damped tele-scopic fork production motorcycle is made. Henne raises the world record to 159mph (256kph).

1936 Tubular frame re-adopted. New *Kompressor* (supercharged) machine takes the racing world by storm.

1937 Henne increases world record to 173mph (279kph) with 500cc super-charged machine.

1938 Rear-suspension introduced on production motorcycles.

1939 George Meier wins the Isle of Man 500cc TT on the supercharged BMW, the Model 255.

1941 R75 Wehrmacht sidecar outfit intro-duced with sidecar drive and reverse gear.

1945 BMW factory devastated by the war and reparations.

1949 The R24, the first motorcycle to be made after the war, enters production.

1950 The first twin since the war, the 51/2, is made using old designs.

1951 The R51/3 introduces the first post-war designs.

1954 The first 100mph roadster, the R68, is launched. Noll and Cron win the first of 19 consecutive world sidecar championships won by BMW-mounted sidecar riders.

1955 The all-pivot framed BMWs, derived from the previous year's racing machines, are launched. They have swinging-arm rear-suspension and leading link front-forks.

1961 The MLG-prepared R69S breaks the world 24-hour speed record.

1969 A complete new motorcycle is launched: known as the /5 series, it includes the first production 750cc machine since 1941.

1973 A 900cc BMW is made, the largest and fastest ever road bike.

1976 The first BMW with a full fairing, the 1,000cc R100RS is offered for sale.

1978 Introduction of the R100RT, a fully-faired touring version from the 1,000cc range.

1983 For the first time since 1923 BMW launch a totally new motorcycle, the water-cooled K series.

1988 BMW produce the first ever production motorcycle with anti-lock brakes.

1989 Another radical departure, the futuristic 16-valve K1 appears. It has a top speed of over 140mph (225kph), the fastest road-going BMW made.

1990 Four-valve K series four introduced. R100GS Paris–Dakar launched.

1992 K1100LT made.

1993 K1100RS made.
New generation boxer, the R1100RS launched, soon followed by the R1100GS.
The first single for nearly thirty years, the F650 Funduro, is made.

1994 A smaller version of the new generation boxer, the R850, is made; at the same time a naked 1100, the R1100R, is announced.

1995 Top of the range R1100RT is launched.

Foreword

There is no more interesting story in the motoring world than that of BMW. From early days as aircraft engine manufacturers – the familiar blue and white badge represents a spinning propellor – to road transport, the BMW motor car and motorcycle have always been complementary to one another. From 1923, motorbikes provided the mainstay of BMW and kept the company going until 1961 when the car side started its own success story. It has since become the dominant partner.

My friend Bruce Preston has written the story of BMW, covering eighty-five years of development. There is no one more suited than him to the subject, for he is an enthusiastic biker of very great experience and a journalist of repute. He rode from the Arctic Circle to Gibraltar in ten days, and travelling 1,000 miles in a day required not only dedication but a strong sense of humour as well! Both these journeys were on BMWs which were very suitable for the task: the marque has built up an excellent reputation for comfortable and reliable long distance touring.

I have been a keen motorcyclist for many years so I am particularly pleased to write the foreword; I own a K100, Isetta and 735 Series car, so enjoy BMW on two, three and four wheels.

When the new K100 liquid-cooled in-line four-cylinder appeared in 1983, many thought that it would be the death knell of the Boxer-twins, but thankfully this didn't happen and the twin-cylinder machines in various guises account for forty per cent of the BMW production at Spandau.

I still derive pleasure from riding the Boxer-twins. It is remarkable that the original concept of a horizontally opposed two-cylinder engine and shaft-drive should still be with us today, and I much enjoyed following its development through the pages of *BMW*.

Motoring books come in various styles: either endless pages of facts and figures or a text containing too little. Bruce Preston has struck a happy medium in *BMW*, so that it is most readable from beginning to end. Obviously his heart is in the subject, for he has been riding BMWs as personal transport for the past thirty years and looks all set to continue doing so for a long time to come.

Lord Strathcarron

1   A Flying Start

Any vehicle leaving the BMW production line today, whether car or motorcycle, carries a graphic reminder of the original direction of the company, in the shape of the blue and white quartered badge which represents a spinning propellor. This symbol is entirely appropriate as, before the introduction of the name BMW, the company was known as Bayerische Flugzeugwerke (Bavarian Aeroplane Works).

To give a true historical picture of the beginnings of BMW we need to go back to 1916 when two well-established Munich firms, Rapp Motorenwerke GmbH (founded by Karl Rapp in 1913) and Gustav Otto Flugzenmaschinenfabrik (a company started by Gustav Otto in 1911 to make aeroplanes) formed BFW with a stock capital of 200,000 Reichsmarks. The date was 7 March 1916. The Managing Director was Karl Popp. (Gustav Otto was the son of Nicholas Otto, who gave his name to the Otto-cycle, which is the principle upon which the four-stroke engine works.)

BFW's intention was to produce a complete aircraft, and a new factory was built alongside Munich airfield, next to the Otto works. (This is in the same part of Munich that still houses the major BMW factory today.)

Both companies provided men of outstanding ability. Rapp brought to the operation a man named Max Friz. Friz joined the company in 1914 and soon earned a reputation as a fine engineer. His designs for a six-cylinder in-line overhead camshaft aircraft engine were eagerly accepted by the German government of the day, and soon a large order was placed (remember that this was during World War I). Only seventy examples had been delivered before the war ended, one satisfied user being the legendary Von Richthofen (the 'Red Baron').

The name BMW (Bayerisch Motoren Werke) GmbH was introduced in 1917 just a year after BFW's formation. In 1918, *Aktiengesellschaft* (AG) – public company – status was granted. Soon the disastrous World War I ended and the peace treaty severely curtailed the activities of German industry. No light aircraft or engines could be made. That, at least, was the edict of the Allies, but Max Friz thought otherwise and secretly prepared an aeroplane using the six-cylinder in-line BMW engine. The six was installed in a BFW biplane and astounded the aviation world by climbing to 32,000 feet (9,754 metres) – a world record height at that time, which so incensed the Allies that they confiscated all plans and documents relating to it. Even if the newly formed BMW had not planned to move into the world of motoring, they would have had little other choice given the circumstances.

Times were hard and things looked black at BMW. It was Managing Director Karl Popp who found a life-saver in the shape of a Viennese banker with an Italian name, Camillo Castiglioni. The company was reformed with a stock capital of twelve million Reichsmarks and Castiglioni as the major shareholder. It was not the first time Castiglioni had been involved: he had provided the financial backing for the formation of BFW and again in 1917.

Another director was Fritz Neumeyer, a name that was to become better known when he founded the Zundapp concern.

Even so, BMW were in dire trouble. A new factory had been built for aircraft manufacture, the larger part of which was shut down; the staff was reduced from a wartime high of 3,500 employees to just a handful and the offices and canteen were closed. Existing stocks were scrapped, often being melted down to obtain raw material.

In 1921 the remaining workforce was kept occupied by a welcome contract, arranged by Castiglioni, to make air brakes for trains and agricultural machines, and castings for other companies. Tin and plywood remains of the aircraft were used to make office furniture and tool cases. The air brakes were for Kunze-Knorr-Bremese AG, another company with which Castiglioni was involved. As a major contractor Kunze-Knorr-Bremese acquired ninety per cent of the stock capital.

Franz Joseph 'Karl' Popp

Popp was the guiding light of BMW from its formation. He graduated in mechanical and electrical engineering in Bruenn and served in the Austrian/Hungarian wartime navy in Poland, joining the reserve in 1915. After a spell with AEG the Viennese-born Austrian was seconded to Astro/Daimler in Vienna Neustadt. He joined BMW in 1917 and became General Manager.

His real strength was as a leader and he moulded together a young, energetic team of engineers to work to a standard that was normally only associated with the aircraft industry. He remained as General Manager until 1942, having guided the company through the ravages of World War I and seen it become one of the world's great motorcycle and aircraft engine manufacturers.

The only other work available for the BMW factory was the manufacture of a water-cooled engine for lorry and marine use and a motorcycle engine. This was really the beginning of the BMW motorcycle story although it is doubtful if anyone involved at the time could have foreseen how it would turn out. Engines were made for the still-functioning Otto factory next door. Otto, who must have been in as much financial trouble as BMW, had become involved in motorcycle production when they acquired a small Munich company which was making a machine called the Flink. The Flink, a 148cc three-port two-stroke was made at 76 Neulerchenfelder Strasse. It was a straight-forward lightweight using a Kurier engine that is of interest only because it might have provided the impetus for BMW, by way of Otto, to get involved in motorcycling.

It is at this stage that one of the great academic motorcycling arguments probably originated. I am indebted to Joe Greenwood, author of 'In Search of BMW', serialised in the *BMW Club Journal* from 1979 to 1982, for allowing me to quote his interpretation of the events that have caused many motor-cycling historians to write confidently that the BMW was really a Douglas made under licence. A similar accusation concerning ABC was to follow a few years later.

BMW were contracted to make a 500cc side-valve flat-twin, initially for Otto. It was known as the M2B15 (the designation was arrived at quite simply: the M meant motor, the 2 the number of cylinders and the B was for boxer). It was a 494cc engine with a bore and stroke ratio that was absolutely 'square', 68×68mm. Known as the Bayern-Kleinmotor, it produced a modest (by today's standards) 6PS – PS = *Pferdestärke* = .986 horsepower. Series production started in 1922, the year in which BMW purchased the property of Bayerische Flugzeugwerke AG in Lerchenauer Strasse, Munich, for seventy-five million Reichsmarks.

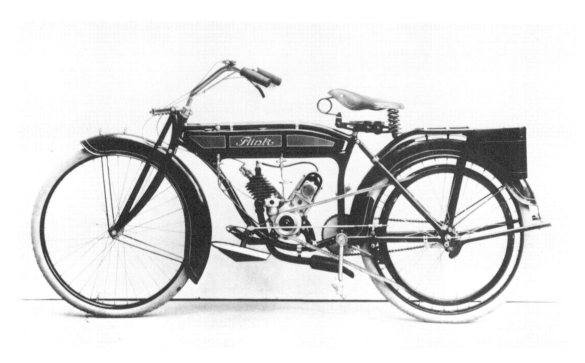

The Flink, the motorcycle that first attracted the interest of the company that was to become BMW.

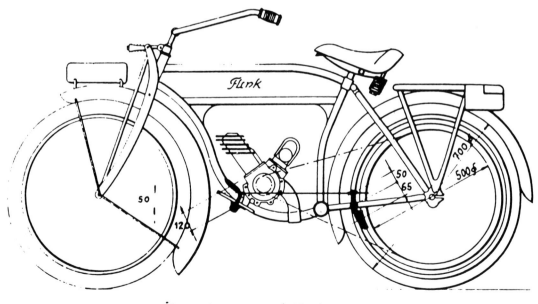

Übersetzungsverhältnis: 1,3 : 1

The Flink – the original involvement of BMW's predecessors in motorcycling.

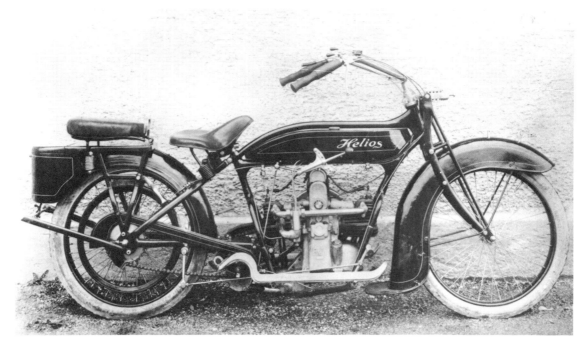

The Helios – one of many machines that used the 486cc BMW M2B15 engine.

The M2B15 was available, in much the same way as the JAP engine was in England, for fitting to proprietary manufacturers' products. It was first used in the Helios (made by Otto), and then by numerous other makers including six smaller German manufacturers: the Nürnberg-based Victoria company; Corona; Heller; Scheid; Henninger and SMW. Even a long-forgotten (except by the historians) Austrian make, Bison, used the engine.

Fairly soon BMW took over Helios production, and with it the licence granted by the British manufacturer Douglas to make the fore-and-aft horizontally opposed engine. This licence was commonly thought to be held by the Gustav Otto works, trading under the old BFW title. That the engine was an original Douglas design there seems to be little doubt, but it is equally certain that it never appeared with a BMW badge on the tank.

Max Friz was not exactly overjoyed at the prospect of becoming a motorcycle designer. His love was aeroplanes and, had it not been for the restriction on their manufacture, it is doubtful whether he would ever have turned his hand to motorcycle engines. Karl Popp, aware of the need for a better engine than was currently available, prevailed on him to design a new improved one. Reluctantly, Friz agreed and sat down to design what was to become one of the classic engines in motorcycling: the BMW boxer motor.

THE R32

Germany in the early 1920s was in a state of trauma. Inflation was at a level that makes today's figures seem acceptable; the country was devastated by the war and the reparations that followed; and there was no money around for luxuries like motorcycles. Except that to those who purchased them they were not luxuries, they were a lifeline. Remember that there were hardly any cars in the country and, for those who needed to get about, the motorcycle might have been seen as the only way. Over eighty per cent of BMW sales were to business customers. Having said that, BMW then (as now) had set a standard of excellence that they would not compromise in the interests of economy.

The BMW experience with the M2B15 must have been a stimulating one, for they went back to the drawing board to design a new engine. Max Friz, the reluctant motorcycle designer, had learned many lessons with the M2B15, and in designing the new BMW he created an engine that was immediately acknowledged as a classic. An across-the-frame boxer (flat-twin), it bore a superficial resemblance to the Douglas design that it was going to replace; but there the similarity ended.

Friz had his own ideas and from his drawing board came a design that was to set

---

Max Friz

Doctor of Engineering Max Friz joined Rapp as Chief Design Engineer in 1914. His speciality was designing aircraft. When Rapp combined with Otto and became BFW he continued to design aeroplanes but the end of the war meant there was no longer any need for these. He maintained his involvement, though, and in 1919 designed a BMW-engined aircraft that achieved a world altitude record of 32,000 feet (9,754 metres). He designed a butterfly valve for this engine which gave it the edge over its competitors. Friz designed both the six- and twelve-cylinder aircraft engines and these set a total of ninety-eight world records.

He then brought his considerable talents as an aircraft designer to bear on motorcycles. Not satisfied with the Helios' engine, he designed the first-ever BMW motorcycle, the R32, a machine that was the forerunner of all air-cooled BMWs to this day.

His contribution to the success of BMW was incalculable and he was a 'motorcycle constructor' from the beginning of his involvement with BMW until his retirement in 1945. In that time he was responsible for many of the brilliant innovations introduced by BMW.

Martin Stolle (above), who with Max Friz was the father of the M2B15 engine.

Martin Stolle with his mechanics and the first-ever M2B15 motor in a Douglas frame.

the pattern of BMW thinking for the next sixty years. The concept was classic BMW: a flat-twin engine with crank-shaft running fore-and-aft. This made it possible for shaft drive to be used efficiently: this ran to a rear bevel box on the right-hand side of the machine. The drive connection was by way of a Hardy flexible-disc coupling – although not every early R32 was so fitted, the first fifty having a rigid connection. Apart from the advantages of shaft drive, there was the bonus of easy rear-wheel removal. Punctures were common and the intrepid traveller would have welcomed such an innovation. BMW were not the first manufacturer to go for shaft drive but they were without a doubt the most successful.

The motor was mounted in a duplex frame with the gearbox bolted to the rear of the engine and a single plate car-type clutch in-between. The layout will be familiar to anyone who has looked even casually at a modern BMW boxer, for it is utilised right up to the present day. It was known as the R32 and the 'R' model designation has always

been used to indicate an air-cooled BMW. The 'R' stands for *Rad* – as in *Motorrad* – which in German means bike.

When one comes to write about something that happened over sixty years ago, the biggest problem is authentic information. Fortunately for students of motorcycling, a great deal survived World War II. It is a testimony to German thoroughness that there is even an original set of drawings of the R32 in existence.

The amount of detail on such basically simple machines is not great but all the dimensions are clearly marked. Designated the M2B32, the engine started life with the same 68mm square dimensions as the M2B15. The initial capacity was 486cc but this was increased to 494cc in 1925. (At the same time the one-piece cylinder head was split, making access easier and introducing a system that has survived to this day.) The compression ratio was 5.0:1 and lubrication was by forced-feed using a geared oil-pump incorporating the wet-sump method – a system that was used in modified form right

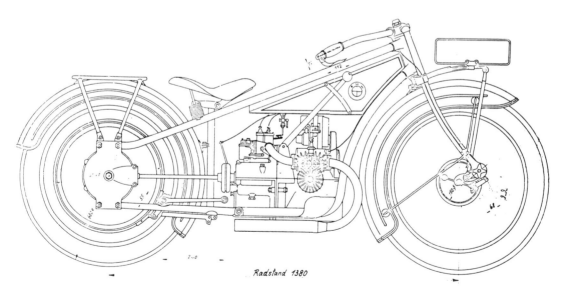

The one that started it all – the R32.

17

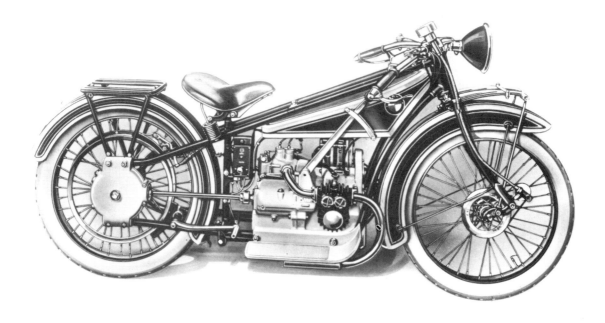

The first complete motorcycle made by BMW, the 1923 R32.

up until 1969. Ignition was by a magneto generator with complicated handlebar controls and, then as now, Bosch spark plugs were used. The lighting system operated by what was called high tension ignition. (Few motorcycles before that time utilised electricity for lighting.)

The three-speed gearbox was grease-filled with a hand-change, as was the fashion of the times. It was to be a little while before the positive-stop mechanism was developed for motorcycle gearboxes. Two rear-drive ratios were offered, 1:4.4 for solo use and 1:5.36 for sidecar use. A single carburettor, listed as the BMW-*spezial*, was mounted on top of the engine and was produced by BMW themselves, who capitalised upon their aircraft manufacturing experience. Twin slides in the one body served the two cylinders.

During the next two years the R32 was produced with little perceptible change but with continual improvement, setting the

pattern followed by BMW to this day. One improvement – doubtless much appreciated by customers – was the provision in 1924 of an internal expanding front-brake. Initially there was no front-brake at all! The rear-brake was known as the wedge-block type. The description suited it, as the rider applied pressure to a pedal which, literally, wedged a block onto a rim bolted to the wheel. It made stopping a motorcycle an interesting experience, the more so before the front-brake was introduced.

Wheels were bicycle-sized, 26×2.5in at the front, 26×3in at the rear, their size being listed in imperial units as opposed to the rest of the machine being in metric – a trend in tyre sizes that has continued, at least as regards diameter. As a matter of interest, the tyres fitted to the machine shown in the publicity shots of the time were made by Metzeler, a company still supplying tyres to BMW as original equipment. A geared drive

The engine of the first ever built R32.

for the handlebar-mounted speedometer was incorporated in the front-wheel.

When compared with the tank bag of a modern motorcycle – which provided a convenient reference point when the first ever engine was resurrected from the BMW archives in Munich – the engine seems minuscule. Indeed it was: the R32 had an overall weight of 264lb (120kg). Fuel consumption was listed as being in the region of 80mpg. A fairly unstressed top speed of 60mph (100kph) came from a motor which produced 8.5PS at 3,300rpm. It was not fast but the designers recognised the importance of reliability. Even with its apparently low top speed it was soon gaining success in competition.

CONTROVERSY: THE R37

By 1925 BMW were beginning to flex their muscles. The R32 had earned almost universal acclaim and it was time to show the

Between 1923 and 1926 3,100 R32s were made on the BMW production line.

bike's worth in sporting competition. To do so, they created a racing version – the R37.

The opportunities for technical improvement can be appreciated when we look at the power output of the new model. Using the original 68×68mm bore and stroke dimensions, but with the compression ratio increased to 6.2:1, the new machine produced almost twice as much power as the R32, offering 16PS at 4,000rpm. Top speed was listed as 71mph (115kph); not much more than the R32 considering that there was almost twice as much power. The designers were learning a basic truth that still applies: the power increase obtained can never be relied upon to give a corresponding increase in speed. Even on a racing motorcycle, fuel consumption was listed and this was now 71mpg!

Perhaps 'racing motorcycle' is a bit of an exaggeration, for the machine which was sold to the public really amounted to a tuned R32 with the lights removed. Just 175 examples were made during its two-year production run. However, ten 'specials' were produced for works-supported riders and were quite different. They had a shorter wheelbase, light alloy cylinder heads and twin carburettors.

There was one major change in that the engine was now of overhead-valve design. This caused the appearance for the first time of a proper rocker cover whose style was to be seen on BMWs for some time to come. Detail improvements included separate cylinder heads, cross-finned cylinders and valve caps. The carburettor was now of the two-slide type. The evil little block-wedge rear-brake had survived, but the front-wheel now had an expanding shoe-brake, similar to the one which had appeared on the second version of the R32. The speedometer was apparently not considered necessary. This seems to be a comment on the philosophy of the day – the rider was expected to go as fast as possible and it was better if he did not know just how fast this was!

As with so many 'improvements', there was a weight penalty, and the R37 was now up to 295lb (134kg). It did not deter research director Rudolf Schleicher from riding one with great verve in Wales in 1926, from where he brought home the company's first major overseas trophy, winning a gold medal in the International Six Days Trial (ISDT) – a six-day scratch around the rough roads of the Welsh countryside. Two other works entries, ridden by Fritz Rother and Baron Egloffstein, won silver and bronze respectively. BMW went home delighted to have proved themselves in what was then the toughest test of motorcycling in the sporting calendar.

Winning was to spark off another controversy though. Once again I am indebted to Joe Greenwood for allowing me to quote from 'In Search of BMW'. He says that Professor A M Low, technical consultant to the Auto-Cycle Union (A-CU), wrote a report on the more interesting technical aspects of the entrants' machines and was full of praise for the BMWs. This brought forth a red-hot letter from Greville Bradshaw, freelance designer for the Sopwith ABC, saying that the BMW was being made to his designs without a manufacturing licence. ABC had been manufacturing a 395cc flat twin of a similar design. Bradshaw said that BMW had requested a set of working drawings for the ABC, and subsequently a further set to convert the engine to 500cc capacity. He had supplied both sets in 1922 and had since had no further communication with them.

Had BMW stolen Bradshaw's designs? Not

Rudolf Schleicher

Schleicher became BMW's Chief Test Engineer and Engineering Director in 1923 and continued his involvement with the company until 1960. His first success was to design the alloy cylinder head that was used in the original BMW motorcycle. He not only played a significant part in the design and production of BMWs, but he also rode them.

His forte was cross-country racing and he astounded the motorcycling world by taking the then new BMW R37 to Wales in 1926, winning the gold medal in the International Six Days Trial (ISDT). The time taken for this trip was counted against his annual holiday.

---

according to Joe Greenwood, who says that Bradshaw never backed up his claim with copies of correspondence regarding what went on. He concedes that the BMW had a superficial resemblance to the ABC, but points out that there were far more differences than similarities; Joe restored an ABC to show there were no significant similarities.

The ABC used a total loss lubrication system, for example, and the BMW a gear-type submerged pump. The ABC was chain driven, the BMW shaft driven, whilst the ABC, which was a very advanced machine for its time, had the luxury of swinging-arm rear-suspension with laminated leaf springs attached either side of the seat tube. There were many other detail differences and it is Joe Greenwood's conclusion that the only similarity was the choice of engine configuration.

Bradshaw's accusations were to stay around for a long time, fuelled perhaps by a British motorcycle press that was understandably home-minded. Even today, BMW owners will be told that their machine is 'really a copy of the ABC', usually by riders who have never seen either an ABC or a BMW of the period.

It is not beyond the bounds of possibility that BMW had sight of the Bradshaw drawings and, maybe, used them as a guide to what not to do. To say the machine is a copy would be like accusing Honda of copying Gilera or MV with their 1969 four-cylinder CB750. There are only so many design options open to engineers and, with the knowledge and materials of the early 1920s, these options were limited. Had Bradshaw produced the original letter from BMW requesting the drawings, his case would have been unarguable. It seems strange that he did not.

SPORTING SUCCESS

BMW had hardly started making motorcycles when sporting success came their way. Rudolf Schleicher, who was Chief Test Engineer and Engineering Director, immediately entered the R32 in races in 1923 but, although surprisingly successful, it was woefully underpowered. It became clear that a proper racing engine was necessary. Max Friz might not have had an initial interest in motorcycles but he wanted success, and he and Schleicher started work on a racing version.

Ten machines were initially made. Listed as R37s, they had a shortened wheelbase, chrome nickel steel forks and the first light alloy cylinder head used on a BMW, which was designed by Schleicher. Their efforts were immediately rewarded when Franz Beiber brought the 1924 German 500cc championship home to Munich; BMW had been in business for only a year!

The next two years saw the impressive R37 scoring wins in a variety of competitions. Road racing successes at almost every Grand Prix circuit in Europe became a matter of course, proving beyond doubt that the R37 was a winner. Schleicher showed that he was more than just a good engineer by taking the machine to Wales in 1926 and entering the ISDT – generally considered the toughest reliability event in the world – as a privateer. Before the start, Schleicher had scoured the country without success for trials tyres. He had no choice but to ride on road tyres and astounded the world by winning the top gold medal, one of the great sporting achievements of the decade. This event was almost the property of British riders and, keeping in mind that the name BMW was virtually unknown in Great Britain at that time, Schleicher and his R37 really put the cat among the pigeons.

The works bikes seemed to be everywhere, winning on the track and on the rough. Wins in the hands of Adolf Bartling, Rudolf Reich, Ernst Henne, Toni Bauhofer and Josef Steltzer – who brought further success to BMW by winning the German championship on the 250cc R39 in 1925 – gave the marque a tremendous boost. By 1926 BMW were established as a major manufacturer and as a successful racer. Only 174 examples of the R37s were made for sale to the public during the two years the machine was in production. The initial ten were works machines and the bikes for sale did not have such a high specification.

Friz and Schleicher were quite satisfied with their first three years in competition but they were not the type of men to rest on their laurels and they had an idea that would once again set the sporting world back on its heels.

2 The First Single

In 1925 BMW came up with their first single-cylinder machine, the R39. At this stage they had not rationalised their model designations so as to have, at least occasionally, a passing connection with the capacity. In later years all the 250s had a 2 after the R, such as the R23. The R39 seems to follow a straight numerical sequence with the missing numbers possibly being allocated to prototypes that never went into production.

The R39 was an immediate success on the race tracks and, in the first year of its life, Josef Stelzer rode one to become German 250cc champion. Its reliability was established. Choice of bore and stroke was (presumably) dictated by the R37 which went into production at much the same time, for they shared the same 68×68mm dimensions. It was to set the style for the next sixty-two years, for every 250cc single-cylinder BMW used the same dimensions, although, unaccountably as time went on, the stated capacity was reduced from 247 to 245cc. For the record, a 68mm bore and stroke gives a nominal cylinder capacity of 246.96cc.

For its time it was quite powerful,

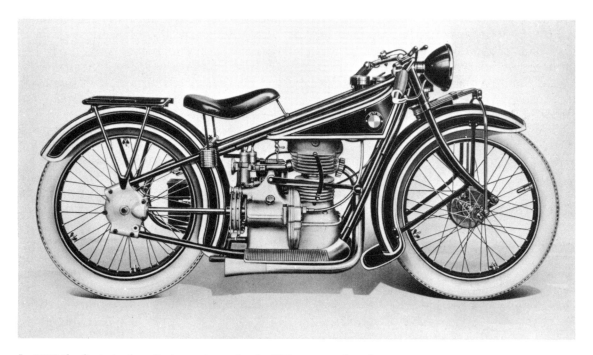

In 1925 the first single-cylinder motorcycle, the R39, was produced.

producing 6PS at 4,000rpm and a top speed of 62mph (100kph), as fast as the R32 and a little cheaper. Few 250s could aspire to such performance; it was not until the late 1930s that British 250s attained such 'over-the-counter' performance.

The basic configuration was faithful to BMW tenets, and archive photographs suggest that the same cycle parts might have been used. Drive was by shaft, as always, but the engine – as was to remain the style for the rest of the life of the BMW single – was placed in the frame with the crankshaft running parallel to the wheels. This enabled a single plate engine-speed clutch to be used and obviated the need to turn the drive through ninety degrees to line up with the shaft. If anything, the singles remained even less changed over the years than the boxers.

The engine had overhead-valve operation, magneto generator, automatic forced-feed oiling by geared oil-pump and an external shoe-brake on the gearbox. This was better than the block-brake but things would not really improve in this department until BMW designers found an economical way of incorporating internally expanding brake shoes into the rear bevel housing. Fuel consumption was stated to be 113mpg and the R39 tipped the scales at 242lb (110kg).

Although it was to be the boxer that made BMW's fame and fortune, the R39 was probably the best 250cc motorcycle on the market during this period. What a pity that very few seem to have survived. Not surprisingly, perhaps, as only 900 were made during its three-year production life.

CONTINUING IMPROVEMENT

BMW motorcycle manufacture during the first four years was incredibly successful. The R32 had won acclaim across Europe; and its racing derivative, the R37, had swept all

before it in Germany. Versatility was important during this period and, while achieving success on the race track, a similar model was winning medals on rough public roads. In the 1920s the term 'trial' was exactly that, and only the fittest survived.

Perhaps a little belatedly, the British motorcycle industry was beginning to realise that motorcycles needed to be more than lightweight bicycle frames with engines attached to them, and there were a dozen soon-to-be-famous marques introducing new ideas and improving old ones. BMW were by now known as quality manufacturers, their aircraft experience meaning that the engineering was to finer tolerances than those normally used by a motorcycle company. Still the improvements continued, and the R32 was replaced by the R42.

A BMW shape was beginning to evolve and the side-valve engine, now designated the M43, continued. The cylinder head cover was thus not so much a rocker box cover as a piece of sculpture, and was to continue late into the 1930s. The machine had no headlight; this was not offered as standard, and had not been on any model up to that time. You paid extra to see where you were going at night!

A 'square' engine survived but the compression ratio was actually a little lower at 4.9:1. Even so the motor showed a commendable power boost, to 12PS at a leisurely 3,400rpm. Not that it did much for the top speed, which was slightly down on its predecessor. On the other hand fuel consumption was improved to 94mpg, which may well have been the point of the exercise.

A cardan shaft rear-brake, introduced on the R39, replaced the block-brake. This was a pair of narrow brake shoes mounted on the gearbox cases. One heel operated a pedal which brought the shoes to bear on the spinning cardan shaft at the gearbox end, where it left the gearbox by way of a large-diameter connection. Such a system must have created considerable stresses on the crownwheel and pinion assembly.

The R42 here is attached to a Royal sidecar. 1926 saw the BMW being put to commercial use.

Once again sidecar and solo rear-drive options were offered. The rider was also now given a choice of wheel sizes: either 19in or 21in at the front, and 26in or 27in at the rear. The weight was beginning to creep up though: the R42 tipped the scales at 277lb (126kg) some 13lb (6kg) heavier than its predecessor. The success of the R47 is illustrated by its production figures, with 7,000 examples made between 1926 and 1928. It sold for considerably less than the 1923 R32: by this time the factory was prospering, as was the Germany economy, and this reduction in price reflected a strengthening of the Reichsmark.

A year after the introduction of the R42 came the R47, replacing the sporting R37. The broad BMW principles were maintained. The motor, known as the M51, had overhead-valves and produced 18PS at 4,000rpm, giving it a top speed of 68mph (110kph). This, too, was offered with solo or sidecar gearing. Once again 'works' bikes were produced with twin carburettors and other refinements, giving a welcome power boost. The rigid twin-loop steel tubular frame, introduced on the R32, was retained. Rider comfort came by way of just two coil springs supporting the seat; an improvement over the earlier model, however, where the rider was much less well provided for.

Development continued and in 1928 the

Joseph Steltzer and Karl Gall in 1927 with their winning R47s.

The R47 (1927) – still to be seen in old-timer events, including some on the race track.

The heel-operated rear-brake operated directly onto the shaft on this R57 and a number of other models in the 1920s.

R52 replaced the R42. Selling at the same price, it offered – unusually for BMW – a long-stroke engine with a bore of 63mm and a stroke of 78mm, the capacity being just a little lower at 487cc. The engine was known as the M57 and produced exactly the same amount of power as its predecessor. The weight was still creeping up and now stood at 335lb (152kg). The front-suspension was becoming more sophisticated with a spring of six laminated plates with shock absorber. Those opting for sidecar gearing also had a double-disc dry clutch.

Naturally, a racing version was soon to follow and the R57 – confusingly using an M59 engine – was introduced. It produced 50 per cent more power than the R42 but, like the road version, used a long-stroke engine. As always it used overhead-valves and, to complement the slowly increasing performance, a larger front-brake was added. This was also fitted to the R52. Still surviving was the cardan shaft rear-brake which now incorporated what BMW called 'Novotex' magnetic drive. It was rightly claimed to be very quiet.

A change was introduced on this model which was to frustrate BMW owners right up to the introduction of the electric starter in 1969. The kickstarter, previously working in the natural position (that is with the foot pushing it towards the back of the bike) was now made to operate outwards: a rider astride the machine had to kickstart it at right angles to the bike with the left foot. It has given many riders a nasty blow on the ankle, and most overcame the problem by standing alongside the machine to start it. Had the word existed then, however, such behaviour would not have been considered 'macho'!

BMW had, right from the start, opted for left-foot operated starter and gearchange. The British industry preferred to use the right side. British riders 'converting' to BMW always complained that such a choice was unnatural but, once the Japanese motorcycle industry chose the left side for the gearchange lever, there was no other option available. Most modern riders have never changed gears on the right side. The gearbox now used oil instead of grease, and the rear crownwheel and pinion was changed from helical cut to bevel tooth. This is still used on present day BMWs.

The end of the first BMW era was nigh and the R57 was to be the last 500cc overhead-valve BMW for some time to come. BMW were never again to make a 500cc side-valve machine. The next decade would see continued evolution of the BMW motorcycle with most of the changes barely discernible from year to year.

SUPERCHARGING

From 1926 on, students of the BMW racing machines – and these included a fair number from rival factories – noticed a drum-shaped housing above the transmission: the super-charger had arrived. It overcharged each cylinder with mixture, force-feeding it and giving it a significant power increase at high revs. Just how significant was soon shown when Paul Köppen won the 1927 Targa Florio, an incredibly tough race around the mountains of Sicily that was to become

famous years later as a major, and highly dangerous, car race. A year later Ernst Henne repeated the success, and Köppen made it a hat-trick in 1929.

The supercharger, or *Kompressor* as it was known in Germany, gave the machines a tremendous edge over the opposition. Good as the BMW was in normally aspirated form, it just did not have the outstanding handling of the British bikes. Although the British bikes were slower there was a gradual improvement in performance and BMW decided that if they could not yet make up ground on the corners they had better do something about it in a straight line.

The supercharger, an improved version incorporating strengthened shafts made of special steel, was made by the Swiss engineer Zoller. It was installed between the carburettor and two long induction pipes and was mounted above the transmission. It was driven by a spur gear from the crankshaft which had a reduction ratio of 1:1:2. Transmission from the crankshaft to the compressor was by an intermediate shaft by way of bevel wheels. Forcing the gases in by this method increased the power of the standard 500cc BMW from 29PS to 55PS. In most other respects the bike was unchanged, although steel cylinder covers were used for streamlining purposes. The 750 showed an increase from 36PS to 75PS.

Just how effective this could be was shown in September 1929 when Ernst Henne, who was already a successful racer, took a super-charged and highly modified 750 along an *autobahn* near Munich and demolished the absolute world motorcycle record, reaching a maximum speed of 134.25mph (216kph). A year later he increased this to 137.6mph (221.5kph). The determination to reduce drag included Henne wearing a streamlined helmet, which was a strange-looking attachment that did little to improve the handling.

From 1926 to 1929 the *Kompressors* were just about unbeatable, winning the 500cc

Edward Kratz winning the 500cc class in the 1930 Schleizer Dreiecksrennen in Germany.

German championship every year and adding the 1927 750cc championship, won by Henne, and the 1928, 1929 and 1930 1,000cc championships to their bulging trophy cabinet. In this period no less than ninety-one major victories and innumerable minor ones were recorded at home and abroad. It could not go on for ever, and the riders who had done so well aboard the *Kompressors* found that they could no longer hold off the superior handling of British machines. It seemed like a good time to call it a day.

THE FIRST 750

Europe had seen the first 750cc BMW racers

in 1926. Ernst Henne, who was to earn a place in the record books a few years later when he repeatedly broke world records for both solo and sidecar classes, is listed in BMW's own fifty-year celebration publication *Weltrekorde Sporterfolge 50 Jahr BMW* as one of many German racers to win 1,000cc races in the years 1926–1929. As BMW do not admit to making anything over 750cc at this time, the probability is that the riders were using 500s initially and, after they were launched, 750s.

In 1928 the first production 750 became available to the customer. In fact there were to be two: the R62 using the M56S1 engine; and the more sporting R63 which came a year later, its engine being designated the

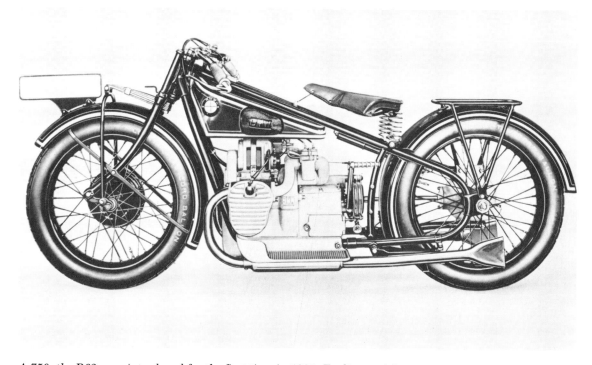

A 750, the R62, was introduced for the first time in 1928. Earlier models used a silencer box under the engine. The silencer on this model was similar to that on the R63, the overhead-valve version.

M60S1. Unusually it was given a name, at least by the British press. In this case it was known as the 'Golden Arrow'. In Great Britain, the price of the R63 was £178.10s, not far short of twice the price of the R52 which sold at £98.14s.

The R62 was an out-and-out touring machine but the customer still had to pay extra for lights! The cycle parts were little changed from the previous models but the new front forks used on the R52 (which was made at the same time) were incorporated. Speedometer drive was from the gearbox – common BMW practice ever since but almost unknown in the 1920s. The bigger machine weighed just over 6lb (3kg) more than the 500 and, in effect, was just a larger engine squeezed into the well-established tubular frame. Top speed was stated to be 71mph

(115kph), but the price to be paid was higher fuel consumption. At 56mpg it was far below the usual BMW consumption.

The R63 differed from the R62 in another way, for where the side-valve machine used square (78×78mm) engine dimensions, the more sporting overhead-valve model settled for a short-stroke variation with a bore of 83mm and a stroke of 63mm. It gave a claimed power output of 24PS at 4,000rpm, somewhat better than the 18PS at 3,400rpm produced by the R62. The side-valve engines had always used cast-iron pistons, whilst the designer of the overhead-valve opted for the more expensive alloy. A higher price-tag reflected the greater sophistication of the R63. It was the fastest production machine made to date, with a top speed of 75mph (121kph). The two 750s weighed the same, and it is perhaps surprising that the side-valve machine was only a couple of miles an hour slower than the more sporting one.

Both bikes still used the diamond-shaped tank, so the easy way to tell them apart was by the rocker box. The R63's is a smooth casting, whilst the R62 cover (which is not a rocker box cover at all) is finned. By 1928 25,000 BMW motorcycles had left the Munich production lines. The vast majority of these were side-valve machines, due to the influence of Herr Popp.

The stage was set for the first world record. This was achieved by Ernst Henne in 1929 when he took a supercharged BMW R63 over the flying kilometre at 134.7mph (216.8kph). Germany already was building *autobahns* and it was on one of these, near Munich, that the record was set. The Avusring, a banked race-track near Berlin, was also used. Henne was to break and re-break the record for many years to come.

Whilst giving considerable attention to their motorcycle business, BMW were also active in other areas. During 1929 they achieved eight world records on land and water. These were triumphantly added to those earned by BMW-engined aeroplanes in the years since 1923, powering Dorniers and Junkers, bomber aircraft that were to become household names in later years – although it is doubtful if British residents will remember them with affection.

In 1928 BMW also produced their first car, the Dixi. It was a name that had been used before by Fahrzeugfabrik Eisenach. They changed their name in 1918 to Gothaer Waggonfabrik and, a year later, to Dixi-Werke. Two years later the Sharipo Group purchased both names and, in 1928, BMW bought the Dixi-Werke, based at Eisenach. It was a name that was to play an important role in pre-war BMW history for it was at Eisenach that the majority of car production was concentrated in the 1930s.

It is interesting to speculate what would have happened had the boundary between the Federal Republic of Germany (FRG) and the German Democratic Republic (GDR) been set just five miles further east, for the Eisenach factory is just inside the (now dismantled) GDR border and is only one hundred miles from Frankfurt. It is reasonable to suppose that car production might have remained there and that of motorcycles in Munich, had the fortunes of war been just a little kinder to the good people of Eisenach. The name was not to be lost, however, and a motorcycle was to appear bearing an EMW badge on the tank after 1945.

The Dixi then being made at Eisenach had nothing in common with the Dixies made from 1904 onwards. This one would be identified instantly by any old-car enthusiast as an Austin Seven built under licence. It was successful in unlikely areas, and won the Alpine Rally in 1929.

Another famous designation became involved when BMW revived the Wartburg name which came as part of the package of the Dixi takeover and was used to identify a modified Austin Seven. Before long BMW were making cars – initially of 700cc – to their own designs and the famous blue and white badge was no longer the prerogative of the motorcycles. BMW continued to grow and there was a massive leap in the number of employees, from 2,630 in 1928 to 3,860 a year later.

3   World Records

Factory support might not have been available on the race tracks in the early 1930s but BMW found a different way of keeping the product in the public eye. They set about collecting world records, amassing no less than seventy-six between 1929 and 1937. It is the name Henne that has been carved forever into the record books, breaking every world record from one mile to 3,000 kilometres, and from one hour to twenty-four hours. Few other BMW riders got a look in.

The absolute world record was raised by Henne every year except 1935, finally reaching 173mph (279.5kph) – after Englishman Fernihough on a 995cc Brough Superior had raised it to 169.3mph (272.5kph) and then an Italian, Taruffi, had taken his Gilera to 169.7mph (273.2kph). Henne made his final attempt on a brand new, supercharged, fully streamlined 500cc BMW and the record was firmly in BMW's grasp. It was to stay there until 1951, for more pressing events in Europe prevented any other serious attempts.

Just to win the world solo record was not enough though. Henne alternated between solo and sidecar throughout the 1930s, the sidecar being little more than a wheeled stick on the side. It was, perhaps, an indication of things to come, for the sidecar wheel was driven, an arrangement that would soon appear on the *Wehrmacht* R75.

A STAR IS BORN

Modern motorcycle enthusiasts tend to think of the pressed steel frame as being inferior to the tubular type, and there are good grounds for this theory. Yet in 1929, when BMW were making faster motorcycles than they had ever done before and when world records were beginning to come their way, they abandoned the tubes and went over to pressed steel, calling it the 'star frame'.

Given today's knowledge it seems an unlikely step to take. Yet it must be remembered that motorcycle design, particularly chassis design, was still in its infancy with no firm tradition or experience to go on. Perhaps the introduction of the R63 and its 24PS power output induced greater stresses than the tubular frames of the day could manage.

Joe Greenwood speculates as to whether the weakness in the tubular frame came from the attachment of the rear-drive housing: it was held by two bolts passing through top and bottom frame tubes, and was considered a weak point in the design as the torque reaction of the final drive was in the vertical plane. The *U-Profil* star frame encircled the rear-drive housing, providing considerable rigidity. When BMW reverted to tubular frames in the late 1930s a similar arrangement was used. Incidentally, Joe Greenwood is of the opinion that the name 'star frame' comes from the German '*stark*', meaning strong or rigid.

One would have expected that the machine used for the successful world record attempt would have capitalised on such innovation but Henne's machine retained the original frame. It seems possible that the pressed steel frame was the product of economic

Even in 1929 the engine of this R11 had superb lines.

necessity rather than any technological advance. Bearing in mind that BMW had recently acquired the Eisenach factory with its considerable experience in pressed steel car design, it is possible that the design was used by the motorcycle people in the euphoria of having hitherto unavailable options available. In its defence, it proved to be a strong and enduring frame, quite able to cope with the power output of the machines of the day.

Two new star-frame models were announced: the R11 – with an M56 engine – and the R16, which had an M60 engine. The specifications were almost identical to their predecessors', except that the compression ratio on the sports machine was slightly increased. The pattern was becoming established; the R11 had a side-valve engine, the R16 an overhead-valve one and a more

sporting demeanour. The now pampered customer was given lights as standard equipment with a 30-watt headlamp powered by a six-volt magneto generator.

Although the R11 was listed as producing 18PS – the same amount of power as the R63 it replaced – it suffered a considerable performance loss, now being capable of just 62mph (100kph) – barely more than the 500cc R32 that had begun the BMW series six years earlier. Now, though, the larger machine had acquired more than just cubic centimetres. It turned the scales at 357lb (162kg), some 71lb more than the R32. When it is considered that the original 500 could manage only 8.5PS, it could be seen as a salutary lesson in the penalty to be paid for extra weight.

Performance on the R16 was rather better, its 25PS output giving a claimed top speed of 75mph (120kph). Could it be that the

The R11 introduced in 1929 had an elegant (for the period) Royal sidecar complete with spare wheel. The date of this photograph is 1933.

The Deutche Reichspost used a special sidecar made by Royal.

The 730cc R16. By 1933 it had twin carburettors.

difference in performance was deliberate to make the distinction between sporting and touring motorcycles more obvious? There was a considerable price distinction, too. In Great Britain, the 1929 BMW catalogue listed the price of the R11 at 105 guineas and the R16 Golden Arrow at 170 guineas. That guineas were used then is not so unusual. The surprise is that they are not still used. In the same catalogue the tubular-framed R52 and R57 were still offered, at 94 guineas and 110 guineas respectively.

BMWs were beginning to look like the kind of machine that later generations of riders would regard as 'real' motorcycles. Development continued as it had always done, slowly and with little drama. Five versions of the two machines would be made before the next generation came along. A

single carburettor, a Gavernor, served the R11. Towards the end of its life, in 1934, two Amals would replace it and increase the power output to 20PS. One BMW-*Spezial* carburettor was used on the sports model. This too was adapted to Amal but earlier, in 1932. It boosted the power to 33PS at 4,000rpm – quite a leap. In 1931 the rear cardan shaft brake was beefed up and a year later the shaft was split, separating the crown wheel and pinion from the cardan shaft by a short stub.

The three-speed hand-change gearbox (still with the tools housed above) was retained, as were the gear ratios used on the machines that had been replaced. The hand-change arrangement had always been fairly ungainly with a long lever finishing in a quadrant below the fuel tank, obliging the

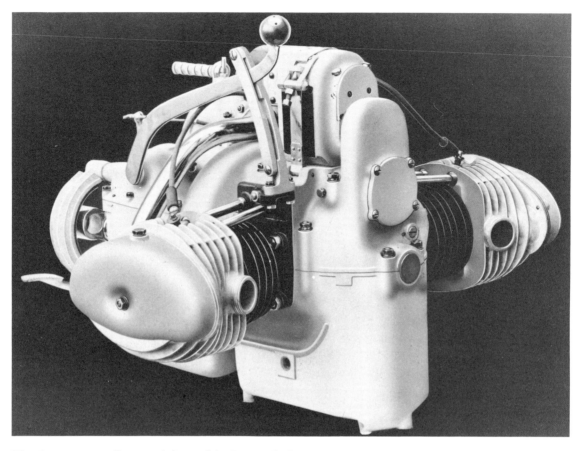

The characteristically smooth lines of the R16 with the gate-type gearchange introduced in 1933.

rider to lean down quite a way to change gear. In 1933 the shift was moved to the fuel tank, neatly recessed into the knee pad. Apart from making life safer for the rider, it gave the machine a much cleaner look.

Changing gear with the hand-change was long-winded enough as it was: the rider had to close the throttle, move his hand to the gearchange lever, pull in the clutch, move the lever to the desired gear and then return both his hands to the handlebars. By this time, forward momentum could well be lost, especially on a touring machine with only 3,400rpm to play with in the first place. The roads of the time were frequently in rather poor condition and one wonders how many

riders fell off before actually completing the manoeuvre.

Modern motorcyclists might consider the single sprung saddle of pre-war motorcycles a little spartan. Consider then the plight of the pillion passenger, who was left with just a metal carrier and, if he was lucky, a cushion strapped to the top. Footrests were not a part of the package but owners, being expert bodgers like most motorcyclists of the era, soon fashioned suitable footrests.

The frame was described as a rigid pressed steel twin-loop with U-profile. The front forks were the same construction as before but now had nine-plate cantilever springing. The tremendous changes to motorcycle suspension, pioneered by BMW, were just around the corner. Meanwhile, the rider had to absorb the road bumps as best he could.

A NEW *KOMPRESSOR*

Things had changed in Germany since BMW had decided to pull out of racing. The Nazis were now in power and they recognised that there was tremendous publicity to be gained for the 'master race' if home-produced machines and riders were to win races. A new BMW racing machine would have to be built – it duly appeared for the first time in 1935 at the Avusring, in the hands of Wiggerl Kraus.

Previously, the superchargers on BMWs had been supplementary units bolted on to their production racing bikes. This was no longer the case, for the new *Kompressor*, the Model 255, was designed from top to bottom as a supercharged competition engine. It was still a boxer but it utilised overhead camshafts, with two camshafts per cylinder,

both driven by a single timing-shaft. The vane type supercharger was driven directly from the end of the crankshaft.

When Kraus wheeled it on to the grid at Avus, the motor was housed in the R5 frame and the new telescopic front forks were used. It soon proved to be incredibly reliable and the machine was used in the ISDT. It showed its versatility by bringing home the coveted trophy, the third successive year it was won by Germany. The winning BMW team of Schorsch (soon to be translated to George) Meier, Josef Forstner and Fritz Lindhardt had been together since 1933 and had earned the nickname 'the cast-iron ones'. Initially it came about because of the iron police helmets that they always wore but their determination never to quit, even if they were, as Meier put it, down to half a handlebar, made the nickname very apt.

It was on the race track that the new *Kompressor* was to find eternal fame, though. In 1937 one was loaned to an Englishman, Jock West, to ride in the most famous race of all, the Isle of Man Senior TT.

George Meier's winning Kompressor *Model 255.*

It was the first ever official BMW visit to the TT races and no more than a proving run for greater things the following year. Even so, the experienced West gave notice that BMW were aiming high and he finished a creditable sixth.

A year later BMW were back in force with a new sprung frame. The racer had shown its mettle the year before when Karl Gall had won the German, Hungarian and Dutch TTs, whilst West had won the Ulster Grand Prix. It was decreed by the political masters back home that a German would win on a BMW and Gall and George Meier – who had been rewarded for his cross-country success by a place in the 1937 race team – travelled to the Island. Gall and Meier had the new fully sprung machine, whilst West had been loaned the unsprung model from the previous year.

Learning the TT course is not easy and West, on the rigid rear-end model, was noticeably faster than the Germans. Meier fell off on his first practice lap and Gall crashed badly, being found lying in water by the next rider along, who happened to be Jock West.

Meier and West were the two BMW starters and Meier rode one of the shortest TTs on record when he was unable to remove the warming-up plugs from his machine before the start. The soft plugs took him less than a mile, so it was up to West to fly the BMW flag, which he did very competently, finishing fifth.

Meier was a true all-rounder for he was also successfully driving a racing car for Auto-Union. He still found time to win the Belgian, Dutch, German and Italian Grands Prix (although the Dutch one was actually called the TT) to become European champion, which he added to the German championship. In effect this made him world champion, although there was no such title at that time. West managed to retain his hold on the Ulster Grand Prix.

By June 1939 the German war machine had already begun rolling, but Gall and Meier again joined West in the Isle of Man for what was to be one last crack at the Senior TT. Gall had spent three months in Ramsey Cottage Hospital after his 1938 accident and it was his tragic fate to finish up there again after crashing at Ballaugh Bridge during practice. This time his injuries were so bad that he died four days later. A plaque to his memory was unveiled at Ballaugh in 1964 by his widow.

Meier and West still started in the race and it was really a procession. Norton had declined to enter a full works team as they were pre-occupied with war work but AJS, Moto Guzzi, Velocette, DKW and NSU all had supercharged racers entered in the TT that year (not all of them in the Senior, and few finished any race). George Meier took the 255 to an easy win at a record average speed of over 89mph (143kph), finishing over two minutes in front of West, who was in second place. A privately entered Norton came third.

It was the last time supercharged machines were to be seen in the Isle of Man for soon afterwards came World War II. Later, in 1947, superchargers were banned by the racing authorities. Supercharged BMWs continued to be seen on German tracks for a while after the end of hostilities as Germany (and Italy) were not invited to re-join the hierarchy. Once they were re-admitted, the day of the supercharger was over.

THE ECONOMY MOTORCYCLE

The year 1931 was not a good time to be making motorcycles. Karl Popp had often said that the BMW motorcycle would never be a machine for the masses but, with seemingly the whole world in recession, BMW too had to look towards the cheaper market. A

198cc single-cylinder motorcycle was designed. An influencing factor was the removal in Germany of the need to pay tax on, or have a licence for, a motorcycle under 200cc.

As a result BMW produced the smallest motorcycle they would ever make, the R2. Not that it was cheap, for BMW seemed incapable of such a thing. The R2 sold at almost half the cost of the big twins and was very expensive for a 198cc motorcycle. BMW were unable to compromise their standards for, although the machine was lightweight, it had the same degree of engineering finesse as the larger models.

The R2 incorporated many of the features of its stablemates. New ideas were tried, too, and, for the first time, BMW produced a one-piece crankcase. They called it the tunnel crankcase and abolished the hitherto normal practice of splitting the unit horizontally. The one-piece crankcase was to be used on air-cooled BMW motorcycles right up to the present day.

BMW produced a single-cylinder engine whose style was to survive right up until 1967, the year the last version was made. An acceptable 6PS was produced by the over-head-valve engine, acceptable especially when compared with the R32 of just eight years before. Initially the valves and springs were exposed but by 1932 they had been enclosed. It had a claimed top speed of just under 60mph (96kph), which was quite remarkable for the era: competitors were struggling to achieve this kind of speed from over-the-counter motorcycles of the same capacity some twenty-five years later. Within two years the power was boosted by thirty-three per cent, to 8PS.

Ignition was by coil, a feature of the singles right until the end of their run. A six-volt generator produced 30 watts: again, not at all bad from such a small motorcycle. Lubrication was by forced-feed with a geared oil pump, another feature established by the machine's bigger brothers. For the first time an air filter was introduced on the single piston valve carburettor, and a single-disc dry clutch carried the power to the three-speed hand-change gearbox. The mechanism for this reverted to a lever running directly from the top of the gearbox with a car-type ball-change.

An improvement was the abolition of the cardan shaft rear-brake, replaced by an internal expanding drum-brake, similar to that used on the front but smaller. The brake was heel-operated, and the footboards used on the larger bikes were a part of the specification. BMW having thrown-in their lot with the pressed steel frame, it was also used on the R2, as were the nine-plate cantilever front forks (also known as trailing link forks). A neat touch was the provision of a front stand to assist in front wheel removal. In keeping with the scaled down requirement of the machine, both wheels were 25×3in. At the very end of the production run in 1936, a dog-driven rear-wheel was introduced, another innovation that still survives on BMW twins. It makes rear-wheel removal easy.

Weighing in at 242lb (110kg) the R2 was only a little lighter than the R32 but had a comprehensive specification – probably the most luxurious available for a machine of its class. The smaller engine and lighter weight held another bonus for owners, in that the bike would do 100mpg. At a time when money was in short supply this could have been important, but the comparatively high price of the R2 would have put it out of reach of those to whom such things were vital. In the six years over 15,000 examples were produced. What a pity so few have survived.

A year after the R2 was offered for sale, BMW went to the other end of the scale and manufactured what was to be the largest single-cylinder motorcycle that they ever made (until the appearance of the F650 Funduro): the R4, with the engine designation of M69S1. Perhaps coincidentally, the 12PS power output of the R4 was exactly double that of the R2, and at 398cc it was pretty well twice the size. It is rare that power and capacity equate so accurately. Unfortunately for BMW, performance did not follow this trend and the bigger machine was just three miles an hour faster than the tiddler. Fuel consumption dropped to 80mpg.

Almost inexplicably, the kickstarter was moved to the right side and worked in the conventional manner. Whether this had anything to do with a growing interest by the military in this model is a matter of speculation, but the kickstarter on all the singles used by the German army until World War II began had right-side kickstarters.

Shortly after the introduction of the R4, the Third Reich was created and Germany began to re-equip its army. It was the good fortune of BMW that the R4 seemed to fit the bill of a dogsbody-bike admirably. A large proportion of the 15,000 R4s made were finished in the German army's olive drab.

Initially the gearchange on the three-speeder was by the original long rod method, but the second model (in a series of five) introduced a four-speed gearbox and a gated gearchange. It was the first machine of the marque to offer a four-speeder for road use.

The pressed steel frame, rigid rear-end, leading link front forks and sprung saddle were still common to all models (although the saddle used similar springs to the ones that were first introduced on the R32) and the R4 reverted to the larger 26in wheels of the twins. The production run lasted from 1932 to 1938.

A smaller stablemate to the R4 was introduced in 1936. It was the 305cc R3 and replaced the R2. The chassis was the same as

In 1936 the single-cylinder R3 was launched, an uprated version of the R2 first made in 1931.

In 1935 the telescopic front fork was introduced. Initially it was tried on the R7, which never went into production. It was many years before customers were ready to accept 'styling'.

that used on the R4, with which it shared the provision of a right-foot kickstarter. The stroke of both machines remained the same and the smaller capacity was achieved by using a 68mm bore. It was a successful engine when one compares the performance figures, for it produced 11PS (the R4 was by this time up to 14PS) and its listed top speed was the same as the R4, 62mph (100kph) with a much improved fuel consumption of 94mpg. Alas, such qualities did not seem to matter much and only 740 examples were made during a production run that was to last just one year.

The final single using the *U-Profil* (star) frame came on the market in 1937 and was called the R35. This shared the 84mm stroke with the R3 and its 340cc capacity was achieved with a 72mm bore. It sold at the same price as the R3, and was listed as having exactly the same top speed as both the smaller bike and the R4. It also produced the same power as the R4 – 14PS – but weighed, at 341lb (155kg) some 40lb

(18kg) more than the bigger bike. The R3 turned the scales at 328lb (149lb).

Much of this extra weight came from what was the greatest step forward yet in motorcycle suspension: the telescopic front fork, first offered two years earlier on the R12/R17 series. The R35 might not have been any faster than the R3 but the handling would have been improved out of all recognition.

This marked the beginning of a new era in motorcycle design, and one that has lasted to the present day. At the same time, it made just about every other motorcycle manufacturer realise that the girder fork was a thing of the past.

THE TWINS ARE UPDATED

The success of the single-cylinder machines was largely thanks to two factors: the R2 benefited from tax laws and the larger singles from the interest of the *Wehrmacht*.

Soon after the R7 came the R17, a sporting 736cc machine, which was the first in the world to offer telescopic front forks.

This meant that BMW had arrived in 1935 with twin-cylinder machines that were little changed from the models introduced in 1928 and 1929. Sales had accordingly suffered and the time was ripe for a revamp.

To be honest, it was not all that much of a revamp, but four major changes were made; enough to boost sales of the new R12 and R17, which replaced the R11 and R16. More importantly these changes attracted the attention not only of the *Wehrmacht* but also of many other Government services, and provided the springboard for further refinement in the years to come.

Undoubtedly the most significant improvement was the introduction of telescopic front forks. No other manufacturer had offered anything like it before and, had it not been for the war, would not have done so for some time to come, as BMW had it tied up with patents. The term 'quantum leap' is

often used to describe fairly modest engineering steps. It applies to the introduction of the telescopic fork no more than to any other engineering invention but, by any standards, it was a leap forward indeed.

The new fork incorporated a hydraulic shock absorber and helical compression springs, in essence exactly the same as those used on present day bikes. It was a masterpiece, and the British motorcycle industry could do nothing more than look on in envy. The rider was now able to negotiate bumpy roads without the constant threat of the front forks reacting violently, often throwing him down the road.

One bonus of the new front forks was that wheel size could be reduced, and the two new machines now boasted 19in wheels. In addition, the wheels were now interchangeable, a feature that was of particular use to the sidecar rider seeking to equalise tyre

Twin carburettors were introduced on later versions of the side-valve 745cc R12. It also had telescopic front forks and interchangeable wheels.

wear. Interchangeable wheels were to be offered to BMW owners until the end of the Earles-fork models in 1969.

The new tyre size had also been adopted by the majority of the British motorcycle industry, so there was considerable harmonisation in this areas. This tyre size is used on many bikes today and remained until recently, alongside the 18in tyre, the choice of most bike makers. Another advantage was that the customer could be reasonably sure of getting tyres for his motorcycle anywhere in Europe. (Not that many motorcyclists ventured abroad before the war.) To complete the cycle parts package, the new twins had been adapted to provide an internal expanding shoe rear-brake to complement the front.

Another change much appreciated by owners was the provision of a four-speed gearbox, an additional gear enabling better use to be made than previously of the 18PS (at 3,400rpm) produced by the side-valve R12. This power was soon increased to 20PS with the introduction of twin Amal carburettors (German Amals, made under licence). The sporting version, the overhead-valve R17, was introduced with twin carburettors and produced a hefty 33PS. For BMW it meant soaring to heights previously reached only by their aeroplanes, which had continued to break all records. Reaching 5,000rpm, the highest yet by a BMW road bike, the R17 was capable of 87mph (140kph). Inevitably, it seems, the weight was still creeping up, an indication of the increasing sophistication of the machines. The R12 now tipped the scales at 407lb (185kg), an increase of 50lb (23kg) over the R11 – there was a price to pay for telescopic front forks. The price was not in Reichsmarks though, for the cost of the R11 and R12 were exactly the same.

Both models used the same pressed steel chassis as their predecessors and both used basically the same engine. For all the additions, the new models were very much developments of the older ones and the time was ripe for a major design exercise.

43

4 A New Generation

In 1936 a completely new 500cc BMW, their first in this capacity since 1930, arrived on the market. Its design specification was far in excess of most other machines in the world. It was known as the R5 and is still thought of by many enthusiasts as being the best machine made in the 1930s; the world's press went overboard for it. The R5 was the forerunner of a series of new models that would be introduced in 1937. It was also the first twin where the model number actually indicated the capacity. In future most BMWs would have the same logical identification, although the company still deviated occasionally lest anyone should think that they were conforming.

The R5 was probably the most innovative motorcycle in the world at the time and featured the hydraulically damped telescopic front forks introduced the year before on the 750s, but with the addition of a steering damper. It was totally different from any previous BMW and saw the company reverting to a tubular frame – more than that, the tube tapered from circular to oval. Just how this was achieved has puzzled historians ever since. One suggestion is that the R5's designer, Rudolf Schleicher, learned the trick whilst on secondment to Auto-Union in the early 1930s. It was a characteristic that survived right up to the arrival of the /5 series BMWs in 1969. The old 'star frame' would survive until 1940 on the R35 but, from 1936, BMW would never again produce a pressed steel frame twin for public sale.

The new frame, which was common to the increasingly successful racing machines (which are dealt with later on) was of the twin-tube cradle type, with the arrangement introduced on the pressed steel frames of the rear-drive being encompassed in the frame tube by a circular loop, thus offering essential rigidity where the shaft drive was causing most stresses. The frame was welded and bolted and described as a closed triangle twin-loop.

But there was much more to the new machine than new cycle parts. Of greater technical interest was the engine. It is not the intention of this book to delve too deeply into the mechanical internals of various BMW models, lest it should become no more than a technical treatise. However, because the R5 differed so radically from previous twins it is worth looking a little deeper into its specification.

The crankcase was of the 'tunnel' type, the one-piece previously used only on the singles. Such engineering needs the kind of expertise and equipment that few motorcycle manufacturers had available and BMW scored there because of their aircraft experience. Until this time, production of the overhead-valve BMW twins had utilised just one camshaft with cams operating valves on both sides. The R5 had a more complicated arrangement where each cylinder had its own camshaft incorporating a gear on each. A further gear above the camshaft gears served the dynamo and, below, a gear on the end of the crankshaft completed the design, the whole assembly being chain-driven. The right-hand camshaft incorporated the

One of the most successful BMW engines, the 1936 494cc R5.

crankcase relief valve and drove the oil pump by way of an inclined shaft-and-worm gear. The other camshaft was home for the two contact breaker cams.

The result was shorter pushrods and a more efficient engine. The R5 accordingly produced 24PS at 5,800rpm, giving it a top speed of 87mph (140kph), a considerable increase on the 71mph (114kph) from the last 500 twin, the R57 of 1930. Comparing photographs, the older model looks just what it is, a motorcycle from the 1920s, whilst the beauty of the R5 did not begin to fade until the Japanese took over in the 1960s. Of course, to many BMW enthusiasts it never has.

The innovations on the R5 were many. The

ignition was by coil served by a dynamo and battery. The latter was located alongside the left-foot-operated transverse kickstarter. Riders were treated to the luxury of a rubber-covered lever on the kickstarter, a pleasure denied in later years. A handlebar-mounted lever gave a useful amount of advance and retard. (Bosch produced the system and it was the first of its type on a BMW twin, although a similar system had been used on the singles.) Hairpin valve springs were used for the first time on a production BMW and two rows of needle rollers were located in each rocker, with independent lubrication to the rocker housing. There is a filler in the top of each rocker cover.

Another innovation for BMW was the

A postitive stop foot-change gearbox was used for the first time on a production BMW when the R5 was launched.

A steering lock was unusual in 1936. The aperture for this can be seen between the handlebars and the headlamp. Note the spring tensioner on the left-hand fork leg.

provision of a positive stop foot-change. The left-side mounted lever shared a common mounting point with the footrest, with a rear-facing lever and a long linkage back to the gearbox. In its way, the new gearchange was as significant to riders of the day as the electric starter would be decades later.

Riding a machine with a hand-change might be considered an art form but to be honest it is an agony. Not surprisingly riders welcomed the idea of a decent foot-change, pioneered by Velocette and introduced on production models in 1934.

So as not to completely abandon tradition, BMW retained what could be considered a kind of hand-change arrangement: a short lever on the right side of the gearbox. Its most useful function was as a neutral finder, for at the time of its introduction BMW did not approve of 'changing down through the gearbox', maybe considering that such behaviour was not seemly and possibly saddling the BMW owner with a staid image that has stuck to this day. He (for there were few 'shes') was expected to glide decorously to a halt and then find neutral, which was all very well unless the rider suddenly wanted to regain forward motion with the machine still in a high gear.

The auxiliary gear lever survived until the introduction of the Earles-forked models in 1955. The author had only one occasion to use it seriously whilst riding a sidecar outfit home, having sprained his left ankle. A kind of gearchange could be managed by reaching down, moving the lever forward and hoping (because there was no positive stop) to find the right gear. It is not a practice to be recommended in today's traffic conditions!

Gone were the footboards, with BMW joining the majority of other makers and providing footrests. These came with serrated teeth allowing for some adjustment to suit the rider.

Another welcome innovation was the

The much-loved Pagusa sprung saddle.

sprung saddle. Made by Pagusa, this was a much underrated feature with the rubber saddle pivoting from the base of the tank on a centre spring. It offered nearly four inches of progressive action, giving a surprisingly high level of comfort. Adjustment could be made to suit the rider's weight. It survived until 1956 when a dual seat was made a standard feature, but there are still riders around who prefer the comfort of the sprung saddle, which is much sought after today by discerning owners of old BMWs. The sprung saddles were indeed very comfortable, but in the author's own experience they had one major disadvantage. The single sheet of rubber was all that separated one's posterior

Even BMW could pull the occasional stunt. This one on an R5 was outside Simpsons in London's Strand. Presumably any spectators were well hidden!

from fresh, cold air: in cold weather it was possible to get a frozen backside.

One thing that did survive on the R5 from the earlier design was the 'reverse' handlebar levers, with their pivot point at the end of the handlebars. They had two advantages. The cable could be given a neat, clean run inside the handlebars, emerging in the centre to run to clutch and brake, and perhaps an even more practical aspect was that the lever-end pointed inwards and was therefore less inclined to impale the rider in the event of spill.

It was many years before ball-end levers became a standard feature on road bikes, even though they were a requirement on

racing machines some time previously. Was it fashion that dictated the fitting of handlebar levers in the now traditional place with the lever pointing outwards? One advantage of the current position is improved leverage, but on balance the old position seems to have much to offer. A single-plate dry clutch was also retained, as were the front and rear drum-brakes.

Interestingly the R5 was slightly cheaper than the R57 introduced six years before, and sold in Great Britain at £115. This is not entirely what it seems, though, for by now the Third Reich was getting the economy and everything else in Germany under control and the Reichsmark was more stable.

At 363lb (165kg) the R5 weighed in at 33lb (15kg) more than the R57. The R5 weighed just 100lb (45kg) more than the R32 introduced thirteen years previously, with performance seeming to have improved by almost the same proportions. Considering the increased weight and power, it is surprising that the claimed fuel consumption was a little better at around 95mpg – a figure that was uncharacteristically optimistic.

The whole machine came across as a 'money no object' exercise, and it is hard to escape the notion that it was part of a grand design where all things German would be presented to the rest of the world as approaching perfection. Whatever the political implications, there can be no doubt that motorcyclists were being given an opportunity to own a machine that today's testers would describe as 'state of the art'. Indeed it was, but the next four years would see further improvements whilst the name BMW would become synonymous with quality and performance.

THE FIRST 600

With the arrival of the R5 it was inevitable that a side-valve version should be introduced. Side-valve engines were considered better for sidecar use, although right from the start all BMW twins and some of the singles had been offered with the option of sidecar or solo gearing, as previously mentioned.

In 1937 came a new capacity for BMW: that of 600cc, a class that would prove popular for some time to come. First to appear was the R6, a 596cc side-valve machine that used exactly the same cycle parts as the acclaimed R5. It shared many features with the 500, including a four-speed foot-change gearbox, telescopic front forks, and coil ignition. What it did not share was

the twin camshafts, as the location of the valves was unsuitable. It was rather cheaper than the more sporting 500 and produced a modest 18PS at 4,800rpm, little more than the R57 of twelve years before. The comparison is misleading, though, for the whole concept of the side-valve engine was one of low-down power and the ability to develop the kind of torque needed to haul a sidecar.

Only 1,850 model R6s were made during its brief life, for a year later the next stage in the continuing story of BMW development was reached. It is a model much sought after by collectors, for few have survived.

BMW had entered the international road race scene with a vengeance some time before and, as part of their search for improvement, had introduced plunger rear-suspension in 1937 on their increasingly successful racing machines. Its appearance on production models was guaranteed, and in 1938 the R61 replaced the R6. There was virtually no change except the machine was offered alongside the R51, of which more later, as the first production motorcycle with plunger rear-suspension.

The system used then appears crude by today's standards, for all that BMW did was to build a short telescopic unit into the rear of the frame. This in effect isolated the rear wheel and permitted a couple of inches of movement as the suspension absorbed at least some of the road's imperfections. Clearly any movement of the rear wheel in relation to the gearbox would necessarily involve some flexibility on the part of the cardan shaft, and this was achieved with a straightforward universal coupling.

Another problem then arose, for it was no longer possible to have the frame encompassing the rear-drive. A new housing was created which could accept the rear-suspension units with the frame foreshortened to finish above and below the universal coupling. What at first glance might have seemed simply a matter of building a sprung unit into the frame was, in the end, very much less simple. Its creation would have kept designers and engineers busy for quite some time.

Perhaps this suspension system would not have lasted as long had World War II not intervened, but it survived until 1955 and the introduction of the R50/60/69 series. As there was virtually no serious motorcycle development at BMW between 1939 and 1952 the actual time-span of the suspension was not all that great.

Added to the telescopic front forks, the suspension now available was still far in advance of anything previously offered to the motorcyclist. It must be remembered though that the BMW then, as now, was an expensive motorcycle. Indeed it was undoubtedly even more out of the reach of the average buyer in the 1930s than it is today and, desirable as all the new offerings were, few could afford them. The new R6 was offered for sale in Great Britain in 1937 at £110 and in 1938 the R71, which was the 750cc version of the R61, at £123. The impecunious but enthusiastic motorcyclist could get a very good motorcycle for half of that: in 1937 the 1,000cc vee-twin Matchless sold for £69.15s.0d.

The R61 remained in production until 1941 and 3,171 examples were made, virtually all of the later ones going to the military or government departments. To this day models are being discovered in the vicinity of various battlefields and a large number of this and other wartime models seem to have finished up in Greece, which has become almost a Mecca for the seeker of old BMWs.

NEW MODELS GALORE

The year 1938 could be seen as the best year for BMW. Six new models were introduced, four being based on the new suspension concept, the other two being single-cylinder models.

In addition to the R61 mentioned previously, the R5 was given the same treatment with little other change and only a slight price rise to become the R51, engine number 254/1. It was a very well made and tough motorcycle and was immediately taken up by the German traffic police. There was one change: the customer now had the option of either the Amal 5/423 carburettors, used on the R5, or the Bing AJ 1/22. It was the first time a Bing had been used on a production BMW, but in time the names would become synonymous.

A 597cc version was also introduced, the R66, with an engine designation of 271/1. Capacity was curiously listed as being just 1cc more than the R61. It was the most powerful twin yet offered to the public and produced 30PS at 5,300rpm, giving it a top speed of 90mph (145kph) and also capable of topping 70mph (113kph) with a sidecar attached. It was the first overhead-valve operated BMW in this class and the gearbox and chassis were identical to that of the R51. Surprisingly, perhaps, the twin camshafts were dropped and a single spur-driven camshaft was introduced, located in the same place as all camshafts on future overhead-valve models up to the introduction of the /5 series. Perhaps the reason for this was the use of the side-valve crankcase, as detailed below.

It is interesting that the Amal carburettor used on this model, more properly called the Fischer-Amal, was designed for sidecar use. One of the problems of high speed cornering with a sidecar outfit is that centrifugal force can starve one of the carburettors of fuel, and the engine will then briefly falter. In this case an auxiliary dashpot was fitted opposite to the float chamber with a small amount of fuel available to prevent this starvation.

The arrangement restricted the already tight space for the rider's foot and it is interesting to look at Joe Greenwood's theories here. He lays the blame squarely on the side-

An unusual R51SS, the sporting version of the R51. This was owned by Charles Lock, former owner of MLG, the London BMW agents.

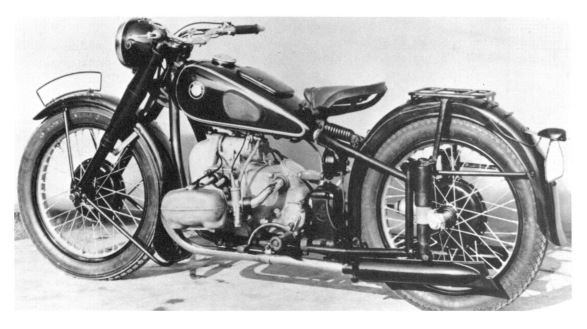

The bigger brother of the R51 was the R66, introduced in 1938.

The last BMW motorcycle with a side-valve engine, the R71. The 1938 model, owned by Franz Marek, has a Rekord sidecar.

valve crankcase. This required a specially designed cylinder using a base exactly as that on the side-valve model, which would have been fine had not the rocker angle then been wrong. This resulted in the cylinder heads – identical to those used on the R51 but machined out to accommodate the larger bore – being unable to locate the rocker spindles quite vertically. The rocker tubes could not be tapered as usual, for extra space had to be allowed to give the pushrods room to overcome the slightly odd angle.

The consequence of all this was that there was even less space for the feet. A moot technical point, perhaps, that most will dismiss as of little concern, but it is Joe Greenwood's feeling that this was one result of the R66 being hurried on to the market. He does concede that owners had little complaint at

such a small inconvenience as the machine was, by the standards of the day, very powerful.

Only 1,628 examples were made up to 1939 with this number dwindling to just thirty-eight made during 1941. The weight, at 410lb (187kg) was 11lb (5kg) more than the R51. The fuel consumption in solo trim was listed at 62mpg, and clearly the day was fast approaching when the 3-gallon (14-litre) fuel tank would need increasing in size.

The final twin to be introduced in 1938 was the R71, a lovely, soft, 745cc machine that produced just 22PS at a lazy 4,600rpm. It was to be the last side-valve engined motorcycle sold by BMW and, arguably, the most pleasing. It was really only intended for sidecar work and was a natural development of the R12, which it replaced. Again it used the gearbox and chassis of the other recently introduced models, although an early photograph shows the machine with the hand-change gearbox fitted on earlier models. Certainly the majority of surviving models used the foot-change gearbox and it is possible that the machine in the photograph was a mock-up.

The R71 had much in common with the other twins introduced that year: the base engine was identical to that used on the R61 and it shared a common stroke with both that and the R66. Yet another new carburettor was used for the R71, a Graetzin-Einschieber of the slide type – as were those made by Amal for the R66.

It was deceptively fast, achieving a top speed of 77mph (125kph) and in Great Britain sold at £123, cheaper than the more sporting R66. Just 2,200 examples were made prior to 1939, a figure that had dropped

to 500 by 1941. Surprisingly, the weight was the same as that of the smaller R66. Perhaps one should not be surprised, for all it involved was a little more metal on the piston and a little less in the cylinder barrels.

MORE SINGLES

BMW launched their last 200cc single, the R20 in 1937. It was a tasty appetiser to the main course. A scaled-down version of the new tubular twin-loop frame was used but the rider still had to contend with a rigid rear-end. Economies had to be made somewhere, for, at £65, the R20 sold in Great Britain for £5 less than the R2 introduced six years earlier. The front forks *looked* like telescopic ones and indeed they were, but they had no shock absorbing, just helical, coil springs. A similar arrangement appeared

Sprung but not hydraulic front forks were used on the 192cc R20.

some years later on the BSA Bantam. It is interesting to speculate as to how BSA came by such a design. That BSA took the basic design of the Bantam from DKW (*Das Kleine Wunder* – the little wonder) as part of the post-war reparations there is little doubt, and it is not unreasonable to suppose that BMW and DKW had shared some ideas in the interest of development.

In their way, the changes made to the R20 were as dramatic as those made to the larger models. The hand-change had given way to foot-change but there were still only three gears (the only single to have four so far was the R4). Although the foot-change gearboxes on the twins were positive stop, meaning that it was only possible to obtain one gear for each positive movement, this was not so on the little 200cc and a road test in *Motor Cycling* (by the ex-Editor, an RAF Squadron Leader at the time) in September 1942 complained of this – he was otherwise fulsome in his praise of the R20. It is a little surprising however, to find a road test on a BMW during war-time!

The now universal footrests were used as was the left-foot-operated kickstarter. A finned silencer was fitted, similar in looks to that used on the twins, and one which also shared the same black finish. Again, a similar-looking silencer was used in the post-war BSA Bantam, but this came much later in the Bantam's production run.

Unfortunately the rider was not afforded the comfort of the Pagusa sprung saddle, recently introduced on the larger machines, although he did have the advantage of 19in wheels. Perhaps, with the rudimentary suspension used, he would have been better served by the larger wheels used previously.

One dubious luxury was a neat tank-mounted toolbox. It would be many years before the safety freaks pointed out that such protruberances were likely to remove the rider's manhood in the event of a sudden stop. The fuel tank looks peanut-sized compared with the twins but actually held only half a gallon less at 2.6 gallons (12 litres). With the engine capable of consuming as little as a gallon of fuel every 115 miles (185km), the bike had the greatest range of any of the models currently available; it is doubtful if the rear-suspension had the same range.

A slight reduction in capacity, from 198 to 192cc, differentiated the R2 from the R20. The piston-valve carburettor used on the R2 had given way to a slide-type Bing-Einschieber AJ 1/20 with simple air strainer, rather than a filter, to keep out the worst of the airborne bits and pieces. Coil ignition was still used with the contact breaker mounted, unusually, on the end of the crankshaft journal.

The internal dimensions of the overhead-valve motor were new, the almost 'square' engine of its predecessor being replaced by a 60×68mm relatively long stroked engine. The stroke was the same as that used on the R5, which suggests that some common ground was found during the manufacturing process.

All these changes made little difference to the performance of the R20, which had the same 59mph (95kph) top speed and the same 8PS power output as the later R2. It allowed much higher revving though, for back in 1931 the R2 had produced its original 6PS at 3,500rpm; the R20 needed 5,400rpm to achieve the same result, although it was much better on acceleration. Maybe the extra weight had something to do with the top speed being unchanged, for the R20 was 286lb (130kg) some 44lb (20kg) more than the R2, although the R2 actually looks heavier. The success of the new lightweight can be judged by its production run, with over 5,000 examples being made in just two years. Few have survived.

It seems that military men the world over have the same reluctance to provide their motorcyclists with the best machinery avail-

The arrival of the single-cylinder R35 in 1937 signalled a buying spree by the German army. Altogether over 15,000 were made, many for military use.

able. There seems to be no other explanation as to why, with all the technical innovation in the models introduced in 1937, a pressed steel framed hand-change 350, the R35, should be in the catalogue.

The R35 was a slightly modernised R4, one concession to comfort being telescopic front forks similar to those used on the R20. The kickstarter remained on the right with a four-speed hand-change gearbox as used on the R4. Even the gearing was similar. Wheels 19in in diameter were another concession to the modern style, whilst the sprung saddle most certainly was not.

With a stroke of 84mm the 340cc R35 engine was identical to the R4 in this respect. It was the longest stroke engine ever made by BMW. The power output, 14PS at 4,500rpm, was slightly better than that of the R4. Top speed, at 62mph (100kph), was the same. It was stated to be a 'cross-country

sport machine' which has more military implications than civilian. Its counterpart in Great Britain would have been the sturdy old 350cc Matchless so beloved of British army despatch riders. During its three-year production run 15,000 R35s were made.

A change in the German tax laws, whereby motorcycles up to 250cc went tax free, signalled the almost instant demise of the R20 and a replacement was soon in the shops. This was the R23, a 247cc overhead-valve single which was merely a bored-out R20. Some detail modifications were made. The lethal lump on the tank that threatened the very future of German youth was recessed, reducing capacity to just over 2 gallons (9.6 litres). Fuel consumption at 94mpg was worse, as was top speed, which was now down to 55mph (90kph).

The performance was not as good, if the stated figures are to be believed, as the 247cc

Franz Marek and just four of his superb collection of BMWs.

R39s that had been available thirteen years earlier. This serves to illustrate just how little importance BMW have paid to top speed, both in the past and, to a lesser degree, today. Their philosophy has always been that it is not *what* it does but *how* it does it that counts.

The weight of the R23 was just under 300lb (136kg). The price was only a little more than that of the model it replaced; its success is reflected in sales of 8,000 during its three-year production run. These figures, as for all BMWs made during this period, were undoubtedly bolstered by numerous military and government orders. It is impossible to use them as a guide to public acceptance.

5 A Technological Wonder

For all the evils of war, it seems that inventors and designers are given time and money to produce things that would have never been countenanced in peacetime. Frequently, war-time innovations live on after the war and benefit society, but all too often the fruits of the inventor's labour wither and die when the perceived need is over. Such was the case with the R75.

First made available to the German army in 1941, the R75 was designed solely for military use by a team supervised by Alex von Falkenhausen and it had little function in an orderly world. It was produced at the Eisenach car manufacturing plant and production continued right up to the end of hostilities in 1945. As this factory finished up in the GDR and records kept during that time have been destroyed, there are only estimates of how long production continued and how many were made. Estimates vary between 10,000 and 20,000. A few have survived and, just maybe, a few more are rotting in some remote battlefield.

The *Wehrmacht* R75, as it was called, was mainly intended for use on the Russian front and in the desert. Indeed the author has a very good friend who was captured by one in the Western Desert, its rider also saving his life by sharing his meagre water supply with him. Many years later the ex-Prisoner of War achieved an ambition and bought his own BMW – this time without the standard machine gun mounted on the sidecar!

The R75 was intended to be more than just a despatch rider's machine. Indeed it was not possible to use it in solo trim, and the R35 did any work where a solo was necessary. Up to three soldiers could be carried, with the sidecar passenger usually in charge of a fearsome machine gun to deal with problems that arose along the way.

Its characteristics were quite different from those required on a road bike, for this machine was intended for both road and cross-country use. Deep-tread 'knobbly' tyres were a standard fitting, with even deeper ones being used in the desert.

As the envisaged terrain for the machine would vary from mud to deep sand, what was in effect a double gearbox was fitted. This offered a choice of four normal ratios and, by stopping and operating a lever hand-change on the tank, the rider was able to select four low cross-country ratios. Two reverse gears were also available by way of a second lever.

It was a rather large lump of motorcycle to have to pull backwards. At the same time the rider could, if desired, lock the differential to the sidecar drive by way of a shaft running from the motorcycle's rear-differential to the side-car wheel. Drive to the sidecar was a simple gear on the end of the shaft driving a larger gear in the hub of the sidecar wheel. Simple: that is, if someone else designs it and shows just how easy it is!

The R75 engine was the first overhead-valve 750 that BMW had made since the demise of the R17 in 1937. The basic design followed the normal BMW pattern of a one-

Built only for military use, the huge R75 featured sidecar drive and reverse gears. This one is painted for desert use and has a massive air filter.

piece crankshaft with camshaft above. The sidecar outfit weighed an incredible 925lb (420kg) so the demands on the motor were far greater than from a normal sidecar, which would have added no more than 200lb (90kg) to the solo motorcycle. Such a great weight needed something special in the way of brakes and the R75 scored another first by having hydraulically assisted ones.

The square (78×78mm) engine had a compression ratio of between 5.6 and 5.8:1 and developed its 26PS at 4,000rpm. It would reach no more than 59mph (95kph) but would pull cleanly with its clutch out at less than two miles an hour.

Naturally the sidecar was fitted only on the right-hand side, which meant that the machine's differential was on the convenient side to reach the sidecar wheel. A spare wheel, which could be used on all locations, was usually carried on the rear. In years to come an almost identical body, complete with spare wheel for all wheels if required, would be marketed by BMW as the TR500. It was actually made by Steib. Whilst not having the elegance of the classic bullet nose Steib, the TR500 was a much more practical sidecar.

The wheels used on the R75 were 16in – the smallest ever to be used by BMW. They gave a lower riding position and lower gearing. There was also the added practical advantage of the wheel accepting car tyres. A rear-drive ratio of 1:6.05 was used, later

Two gearchange levers on the R75 control the high and low speed gearboxes.

dropped slightly to 1:5.69. Compare this to the sidecar rear-drive ratio of the R17 of 1:4.75 (the ratio being the number of times the rear wheel turns in comparison to the shaft) and the machine's ability to dig in and almost climb walls can be appreciated.

Not surprisingly it had its effect on fuel consumption, although 44mpg for road use does not seem too bad. This dropped to 33mpg when used across country and explains the need for the 5.25-gallon (24-litre) fuel tank, the largest yet used on a BMW. A container fixed to the front of the sidecar could be used to carry extra fuel.

A high level exhaust system, with a shield on the silencer to prevent the pillion passenger having too much skin burnt off in the thrill of the chase, gave the outfit the ability to traverse deeper water than would normally be risked. A high level air filter could be added, exiting at the top of the tank, for use in the desert.

Twin saddles offered an ungainly looking but surprisingly comfortable ride. The rider had the adjustable swing saddle similar to that used on the R51 but only with a coil spring, presumably to accept the extra weight of all the equipment he was expected to carry. Perhaps because the technical knowledge of the era did not allow it, the rear-end of the machine was unsprung. A more likely explanation was that no one much cared whether the occupants were comfortable or not as long as they did their job.

Maybe the only older BMW the general public ever sees is the R75 outfit, for no war film is complete without one being either blown up or sent hurtling into a ditch in pursuit of the enemy. Maybe that explains why so few have survived; it is possible that film makers have destroyed more than did the Allies! Whatever the faults of the R75 (and it soon became clear that it was not as suitable as the four-wheel-drive vehicles used by the Americans), the machine had incredible ability to conquer terrain that should have daunted even the most willing motorcycle.

A bizarre episode involving the R75 occurred in 1942 when *Motor Cycling*, affectionately known as the 'Green 'Un', carried a road test of the *Wehrmacht* R75. The rider was Wiggerl Kraus (also known as Ludwig), the BMW works rider who was still employed by BMW in Munich. The report came from a German journalist and even included a photograph of Kraus riding the R75 on the Edelweiss. The story was full of praise for the R75, which it describes as being a seven-speeder, although in fact it had eight forward gears and two for reverse. Just how it got through the wartime censors is a mystery!

THE IRON CURTAIN FALLS

The BMW operation at Eisenach continued for some years to come; indeed the twins which were produced there are still sold in modified form. Production of the twins was moved in its entirety from Eisenach to the Soviet Union and the machine faithfully reproduced to BMW designs. Matching the engineering standards and quality of materials used was not so easy.

The twins have been known by a number of names: first as the Ural Mars M63, then as the Cossack, then the Dneiper, and are also sold as the Neval. It was not badge-engineering by the Soviet manufacturers that caused these name changes: they were made at different factories. Some felt that the quality varied considerably depending upon where the machine was made, but it was more likely dependent upon the quality of the materials available.

Reproduction was so faithful that when the author road-tested the first imported

Ural in the early 1970s an interesting comparison was made. He removed the cylinder head and rocker assembly from his own BMW R60/2 and found that it fitted exactly onto the Ural!

There has always been some debate as to exactly which BMW the Soviets copied. An easy answer is that it is really a combination of the R75 and the R66, with a few modern additions thrown in now and again. Originally the plunger rear-suspension of the R66 was used but, by the time the machine was marketed in Europe, swinging-arm rear-suspension had been added with minor modifications to the original frame design. It looked a little ungainly but worked well enough. Seats from the R75 (and many other BMW models) were identical looking to those used on the Ural, and some sidecar outfits even had the sidecar wheels' drive and a reverse gear as on the *Wehrmacht* machines.

It may be that the Soviet designers increased the size of the R66 motor to 650cc (the size of the Ural) rather than scaling down that of the R75. The Soviet Union has never made any bones about the machine's origins and even the auxiliary gear change lever on the right-hand side was retained. The reason given by Ural for this was that it simplified gear changing when towing a plough or the like. The original concept of the R75 had not been lost.

After 1945 the Eisenach factory continued much as before but just one model was being produced: the R35. Clearly, the factory could no longer be identified with Bavaria so it became the EMW after its home town. The quartered badge was retained but was now red and white rather than the familiar blue and white.

Production of the R35EMW was resumed in 1946, some time before it was achieved in Munich, and continued until 1956 when the factory changed its name. The engine remained the same as the original version, as did the pressed steel frame. There were changes to the suspension with the plunger frame used on the later BMW twins being added and, right at the end of the production run, swinging-arm rear-suspension. It remained true to the concept of BMW design and, doubtless because many of the people building the EMW had previously worked for BMW, engineering standards remained high. A few R35s still survive this side of what was the Iron Curtain but it is not known how many were made or how many still exist in the old East Germany.

BACK TO AEROPLANES

The war clouds that had been gathering over Europe finally rained their hell on the hapless millions. There was little demand for new motorcycles and BMW's production capacity was limited to military machines.

Most workers, and just under 27,000 were employed by the company in 1939, were engaged on producing aircraft engines. The most successful of these was undoubtedly the fourteen-cylinder 810 radial engine with fan-assisted cooling. It powered a squat, almost ugly little fighter plane, the Focke–Wulf 190 (FW–190), that belied its looks by proving to be more than a match for the RAF Spitfires. British designers spent many hours at the drawing board trying to come up with a version of the Spitfire that could match it. This arrived in 1942 and was designated the Mk 1X.

Initially the BMW engine was capable of propelling the FW-190 at 408mph (657kph) but in 1942 a water-injected version, the 810-2D, gave it a top speed of 416mph (670kph) and a ceiling of 37,400 feet (11,400 metres). The Spitfire pilots who had to struggle with a top speed of 369mph (594kph) deserved all the praise heaped on them.

By 1941 there were over 35,000 people on the BMW payroll and preparations were being made for production of the BMW 109–003 jet engine. At the same time production of the R71 motorcycle finally ceased in Germany, but resumed in France in 1945 until 1948 by CMR, and from 1948 to 1955 by CEMEC, later to become known as Ratier. It was to be 1943 before the jet engine went into series production and it almost coincided with the first bombing raids by the Allies on the Munich factory. It seemed unlikely, but in the middle of all this Karl Popp, the first Managing Director and, many feel, its founding father, retired.

In 1939 BMW had production facilities in Berlin (at Spandau, now the current home of the motorcycle factory), Eisenach, and Allach, just outside Munich. All of these were in addition to the main production facility in Munich. Wartime demands had left little resources to make cars or motorcycles and at the end of the war all the factories were, one way or another, devastated. Allach was the first to begin to shake off its despair, repairing vehicles for the United States Army, who had been called in to guard the factory when it was besieged by looters.

Munich had suffered most and the Allies removed just about everything in the free-for-all that followed the war. It might seem a bit harsh looking back over forty-five years but remember that as far as they were concerned this was not a motorcycle factory that needed dismantling but an armaments one. Who can blame the rest of the world for saying 'never again' and determining to dismantle as many of the weapons of war as possible? Inevitably the majority of the records that would have enabled historians to paint a much more detailed picture of the BMW company in the years leading up to 1945 were also lost.

BMW had become experts on jet propulsion and, whilst destroying everything to do with war, the Americans and Soviets were also determined to grab as many of BMW's talented personnel as possible.

Perhaps it was this, or maybe despair, that caused Max Friz to quit. He had designed two advanced aeroplane engines, a twenty-eight-cylinder four-row radial and a propeller gas turbine. The latter was the first of its kind to fly, in 1944. Both had disappeared as part of the reparations, or whatever name one likes to give them.

What happened under the Third Reich is a part of history and there can be no doubt that much of the success of the BMW company in the late 1930s can be attributed to the support of the German political system. That does not detract from their fine engineering skills or their racing achievements.

The 1930s must have seemed a long way away as the war-weary people of Munich began to survey the damage around them. It is, maybe, a comment on the pride of those

who worked for BMW that they drifted back to the factory and, almost with their bare hands, began to salvage something from the rubble. There could have been little financial incentive to do so at that time, for the BMW company was in dire straits.

Slowly, some kind of production facility was created. BMW were not allowed to make motorcycles and, encouraged by the Control Commission (a body that had been created to assist the recovery of Germany), their attention was turned to manufacturing agricultural machinery to assist in feeding the people of a devastated country. Just about the only readily available material was aluminium and the first BMW two-wheeler to appear after the war was an aluminium framed bicycle. It would not have won the the Tour de France but it was a start. It was also

The first post-World War II BMW bicycle made out of scrap metal.

an improvement on the cooking pots that they had previously been making.

It was not long after the war that the prohibition on making motorcycles was lifted for machines of no more than 60cc, which to BMW must have seemed little better than making bicycles. Fortunately, before they became moped manufacturers, restrictions were further lifted and they were allowed to make motorcycles up to 250cc.

A famous name from the past, George Meier, had survived the war and it is he who is credited with helping to guide the factory out of the ruins. The main priority after the war was to manufacture motorcycles to sell to the public.

An interesting postscript to this phase in BMW history is that, with the victors able to appropriate just about any design they fancied, no Western European manufacturer chose to make a copy of the BMW boxers. The Soviets, as have been chronicled, started to make BMW lookalikes almost immediately. The French, too, made a BMW-based machine, the Ratier, but this was under licence rather than being a straight copy.

It was reported that BSA, Britain's largest manufacturer, considered making the R51 but decided that it would be too expensive. BMW had never worked under such constraints. It would be some years before a Japanese manufacturer, Marusho, would make a serious attempt at reproducing the BMW and this was most certainly not a part of the victor's spoils. Nor did it appear to have the blessing of BMW.

BACK TO MOTORCYCLES

From 1948, German motorcycle manufacturers were allowed to make motorcycles up to 250cc. Had the capacity limit been set at 125cc there might have been a very different kind of BMW sold to the public, for an interesting project had been taking shape in the

company's back room. This was known as the R10 and was an attractive 125cc flat twin, with a real change of heart appearing to take place at BMW: this little machine, almost a miniature version of the pre-war 500cc machine in looks, was powered by a two-stroke engine. It was the first time that BMW had seriously dabbled in two-stroke cycle design.

To understand the reasons for this new direction, one would have had to attend BMW's board meetings in Munich. The company possibly feared that the initial 60cc motorcycle limit would be raised only to 125cc, and that if they wished to get back into motorcycling they would have to design something in keeping with their image. Alternatively, the choice of a two-stroke engine could have been influenced by its basic simplicity – which better suited the limited materials available. Fuel quality might also have influenced matters, for a two-stroke would be able to get by on almost any octane petrol whilst a four-stroke might well have suffered burnt valves and even seizure.

In the event, the R10 never went beyond the prototype stage, but the photograph overleaf shows an interesting motorcycle with shaft drive, telescopic front forks and plunger rear-suspension. One photograph also shows what looks like a fire extinguisher mounted under the fuel tank (although BMW Club Vintage Register Secretary, John Laws, who has made some very helpful comments for this edition, suggests that it might be a toolbox). If it is a fire extinguisher it is a comment, perhaps, on the lack of faith in the two-stroke engine! Whether it would have sold is another matter, for the whole essence of 125cc motorcycling is cheapness, and a cheap motorcycle is not something that BMW have ever found easy to produce.

The same argument could be applied to the 250s, yet BMW had long been making high quality single-cylinder machines in this class

By 1948 the R10 was a going concern but it went no further.

that had sold well. Once again there could be a reason, though the rugged lower-powered single would have been ideal for government use and there was a ready market in this area.

When the capacity limit was finally raised, BMW were waiting with an uprated version of the last single that they had made before the war: the R23. Now known as the R24, it looked a much more cohesive machine than its predecessor. Credit for this must go to the redesigned engine which had a smoothness of line not previously seen on a BMW motor-

cycle, and which became the harbinger of BMW style for years to come. The cylinder and head shape was basically that which would be used on the soon-to-be-reintroduced twins.

BMW crankshafts had never gone across the frame on the singles, as was the style on almost all other motorcycles with just one upright cylinder. With the BMW, the crankshaft ran fore-and-aft, which meant that the single plate, engine speed clutch could easily be placed between gearbox and engine. A fourth gear had been added to the gearbox,

A view of the R24.

bringing it into line with the twins, and the layout to the shaft drive could follow the same pattern on the larger machines. Also following the fashion set by the twins was the extra hand-change on the right side. It was essentially a neutral finder but had become a part of the machine's character.

A Bing AJ1/22/140b slide-type carburettor was now standard, the name Amal disappearing from then on from all BMW motorcycles. Coil ignition was still used on the R24 – and continued to be for the remaining production run of all the single-cylinder machines – but the dynamo had given way to a six-volt generator producing 45 watts. Drive from the end of the crankshaft to the camshaft was by chain, with the generator mounted on the crankshaft at the front of the engine, and contact breaker and automatic ignition timing control on the end of the crankshaft journal.

Unusually, the weight of the machine had actually decreased by 11lb (5kg) in comparison with its predecessor and was now 286lb (130kg). There was little change to the cycle

First off the production line in 1949, the R24 complete with the ugliest pillion seat ever made. It also happened to be one of the most comfortable!

65

The tidy engine on the R24.

parts: the bolted-up chassis of the R23 survived, as did the coil spring damped telescopic front forks and rigid rear-end. Riders did not yet have the comfort of the adjustable sprung saddle and still had to rely on two coil springs under the saddle to ease the road shocks. For the first time, the handlebar levers were in the now conventional place with the lever ends pointed outwards. Top speed was a claimed 59mph (95kph), a little faster than the R23. The new engine produced 12PS at 5,600rpm, a 2PS increase on the pre-war version. It also had that extra gear. Interchangeable wheels, for long a feature of the twins, were now used on the singles, too.

Just under 1,000 examples were made in 1948 and the conditions under which they were produced makes one wonder how the craftsmen did it. There were makeshift jigs and tools and a primitive workshop. To those working in such conditions the important thing was that, once again, a motorcycle was being made with a blue and white badge on the tank.

POST-WAR RACING

Following the end of the war there must have been any number of BMWs hidden in haystacks and pigsties. George Meier is credited with the most famous rescue operation, hiding the *Kompressor* in a haystack. A Frenchman, Jean Murit, who had a BMW dealership in Paris, also somehow 'acquired' one of the *Kompressors*. Others, once thought lost forever, just reappeared.

Once the BMW motorcycle production line reopened, the 1,000th R24 was soon proudly leaving Munich.

Meier, having resurrected the 255, dominated racing in Germany from 1947 until 1951. Improvements had been made to the *Kompressor* and just about every German city seemed to have a race meeting. Meier won most of them until the readmission of Germany to the Federation Internationale Motorcycliste, the sport's ruling body.

Other names were coming to the fore, though. Max Klankermeier won the increasingly popular German sidecar championship in 1949, and in 1951 Wiggerl Kraus, the German solo 500cc champion in 1939, achieved the same title on three wheels. Walter Zeller, who had been very successful

racing a normally aspirated BMW, joined the works team and took the solo title from Meier the same year. The incomparable Bavarian had been king for so long that the day just had to come when a pretender would snatch the crown. The new champion proved to be a worthy successor, although Meier came back in 1953 to regain the championship just one more time.

Meier was a superb champion who graced motorcycle sport for twenty years. His reward was a shop just around the corner from the BMW works in Munich. The shop soon became a focal point for all BMW enthusiasts passing through the city. Today

Wiggerl Kraus, who somehow smuggled a road test out of Germany during World War II, racing the Kompressor on the Munich autobahn in 1936.

Walter Zeller, one of the greatest post-war exponents of the BMW, racing to the 1951 German championship.

Max Klankermeier

One of the competition giants in the BMW works, Klankermeier began his riding success in 1934 when he won a silver and special prize in a reliability run through the Bavarian mountains. His real success came after the war when he was German street champion in the sidecar class of 1949, having been runner-up the year before.

Like so many top works riders he was equally at home riding cross-country and until 1954 scored a string of wins in long distance endurance events, winning a silver in the 1951 International Six Days Trial (ISDT). After two years away due to a broken leg he moved to four wheels in 1957 and continued to achieve success when he won the gold medal and was co-winner in the International Austrian Alpine Run.

the name Schorsch Meier no longer appears above the shop, which has been purchased by BMW, but the greatest BMW rider ever is still alive. Given the chance, he will get his leg across a BMW even today, and he took the 1939 TT-winning BMW on a demonstration lap of the TT course fifty years after he first crossed the winning line there.

BMW's interest in racing continued even after they had lost the services of the *Kompressor*, the removal of which cost them nearly 30bhp. Meier rode in the first German Grand Prix to be held after the war (in 1951) and, although he rode as well as he had ever done, the BMW could manage only fifth place. It was time for a new machine.

This was introduced in 1953 when the Rennesport, the RS, was produced. A modified version had been raced in 1952 with swinging-arm rear-suspension grafted to an existing model, but in 1953 a completely new machine was wheeled onto the race

George Meier winning the 1939 Senior TT on the Isle of Man.

Fifty years after winning the Senior TT, George Meier returned to the Isle of Man. This was not his winning machine for the rubber gaiters give it away as a post-war version.

George Meier

Meier's contribution was not so much in the factory (although, like most who worked for BMW, he was a first-class engineer) but on a succession of racing BMWs which he piloted, both off-road and on the race track, with considerable skill. The culmination of his career came when he won the 1939 Isle of Man Senior TT on a supercharged BMW – an Englishman, Jock West, finished in second place on the previous year's model. Perhaps his really great achievement was hiding the TT winning bike in a haystack for the duration of World War II!

After the war Meier continued his sporting involvement and carried on winning races until the early 1950s. He then opened a BMW dealership in Munich which was taken over by BMW upon his retirement. He was still active enough to ride a rapid lap of the Isle of Man TT course in 1989 on his old racing BMW.

track. Two versions were raced, one using conventional carburettors and another fuel injection. Both used the swinging-arm rear-suspension, now in a new frame, and what BMW described as a pivot fork with spring struts, at the front. It was the precursor of the Earles-type fork that would appear on road bikes two years later.

Although the racer was reliable and looked terrific, it was no match for the British and Italian raceware and the only major Grand Prix won was by Zeller on home territory in 1953. Many top riders, including Geoff Duke and John Surtees, tried the BMW. Few mastered it. Dicky Dale won the 1958 Czechoslovak Grand Prix and both he and Fergus Anderson thrilled the fans whilst taking the machines to the leaderboard.

Both, tragically, were killed whilst riding BMWs. The racer achieved some success when a newcomer, Ernst Hiller, won the Austrian Grand Prix in 1958 and Japanese rider, Fumo Ito, gave some great performances, but by the end of the 1950s BMW bowed out of solo Grand Prix racing, never to return. Zeller, who had thrilled race fans the world over, was presented with a 600cc *Kompressor* by BMW upon his retirement.

A different story can be told of the sidecar class. Two Norton-mounted British racers, Eric Oliver and Cyril Smith, dominated the Grand Prix circuits in the early 1950s, but the availability of the RS engine for sidecar racing transformed all that. The BMW boxer engine was particularly suitable for sidecar racing, having a low centre of gravity, plenty

Geoff Duke, one of the greatest road racers ever, on the works Rennesport. Alas, it was not a successful pairing.

Walter Schneider and Hans Strauss waltz to the winning post in the 1955 Isle of Man TT.

of low-down torque and no shortage of horses to give it the racing edge. When used in a sidecar outfit the disadvantage of cylinders sticking out of the side were removed and the days of Oliver and Smith victories were numbered.

First to achieve sidecar success was Willhelm Knoll. Partnered by Fritz Cron in 1954, they took the world championship. Right up to 1974, a succession of BMW teamsters put a BMW stranglehold on the sidecar world championship. Names like Faust and Remmert, Hillebrand and Grunwald, Schneider and Strauss, Fath and Wohlgemut, and Scheidegger and Robinson won the world crown year after year, showing just what a depth of talent there was

in Germany. The greatest of all was Max Deubel who, partnered by Emil Hörner, won the world championship for four successive years from 1961 to 1964, and Klaus Enders and Ralf Engelhardt, kingpins between 1967 and 1974.

One other name should be mentioned, that of the Swiss Florian Camathias. He won more Grands Prix than anyone except Deubel, yet never became world champion. His TT win was an example of the calibre of the man: when his transporter broke down on the mainland, he removed the racing outfit from the vehicle and rode it the hundred miles to Liverpool docks! He was a great character and was tragically killed in 1965 whilst racing at Brands Hatch. BMW-mounted riders won the world sidecar championship for nineteen consecutive years.

Almost as quickly as the BMW dominance of sidecar racing had begun, it ended. By 1974 the sidecar racers were becoming more like racing cars with some very special engines available to those who could afford them. It had been a golden era, but now the name BMW finally disappeared from the Grand Prix circuits.

Racing did not entirely occupy the attention of BMW. In May 1954 they were back on the record run when three riders, George and Hans Meier and Walter Zeller, took a BMW Rennesport to Monthléry in France and averaged 103mph (116mph) over eight and nine hours. Later the same year, in October, Willhelm Knoll took his sidecar outfit (again just a wheel on a stick) to the same circuit and raised the record to 131mph (212kph). Soon Knoll would return with Schneider and

Hillebrand to set a world 24-hour sidecar record at an average speed of 88mph (143kph).

Walter Zeller made the last official works record attempt in October 1955 on an *auto-bahn* near Munich. He made the attempt riding a fuel-injected Rennesport, and he averaged 144mph (233kph) over ten kilometres from a standing start, raising this to 150mph (242kph) over ten miles. Once again Knoll followed Zeller and, using a Rennesport engine that developed in the region of 80bhp running on a mixture of nitromethane and alcohol, set world records ranging from 174mph (280kph) over the flying kilometre to 171mph (276kph) over five miles. It was less than one kph faster than Henne's 1937 world record, but Knoll used a conventional racing sidecar outfit and did not have the benefit of a supercharger.

6 The Twin Reappears

Those who expected the BMW twin, when it reappeared in 1949, to be just a re-hash of the pre-war version were to be disappointed for its motor was considerably changed from the one that had powered the R51. Perfectionists complained that Karl Popp's 'only the best is good enough' philosophy had finally been abandoned, for the new engine had certainly cut a few corners. Not surprisingly, perhaps, for there was still a chronic shortage of quality materials and the price of the new BMW was sky-high. Tariffs included, it sold in Great Britain at over £600 and only the really dedicated could even think about buying one. At today's prices this would buy two top-of-the-range K110LTs!

Why was it considered a compromise? Perhaps the most criticised change was the locating of the rear main bearing directly into the crankcase. Previously it was in its own housing and when the inevitable wear occurred it was just a matter of replacing the bolted-on housing. This had been the practice on pre-war machines and would be reintroduced when the Earles-type models were made.

Until then, owners had a problem. All too soon, rear main bearings would start spinning in their housing, and as this was actually the crankcase the damage was almost irreversible. The author owned one such engine and expected to have to replace the bearing (and all the others!) about every 10,000 miles.

There was also what was known as the centrifuge system used to lubricate the big ends. Oil was circulated around the motor by force-feed with circulation by a geared pump. Feed to the big ends was by 'thrower plates' where the oil was literally thrown from recesses in metal plates bolted onto the crankshaft. It worked very well when new but in the immediate post-war years the quality of both fuel and oil was far below what it is today. Centrifugal action of the thrower plates would separate the unburnt particles from the oil and fill up the plates to the point where they were completely full and the oil supply to the big ends would be cut off. As a result their failure was inevitable.

It was generally accepted in later years that it would take about 50,000 miles (80,500km) for the plates to become clogged. BMW owners of the day constantly agonised over whether it was better to strip and rebuild the engine before the 50,000-mile danger level was reached, with the inevitable cost, or whether to press on and offset the cost of a new crankshaft as well against the hope that it would be longer before a rebuild was necessary.

The author's 1964 R60/2 has done just 51,000 miles; the engine might be removed one day and the thrower plates replaced. It is not a job that can be done without the use of special tools. Fortunately, the BMW Club owns all the necessary tools, which are available on a hire basis (*see* Useful Addresses, page 172).

There were a number of other changes. The cylinder heads now used just four studs for fixing (five had been used previously) but the six-stud cylinder-base flange fitting was

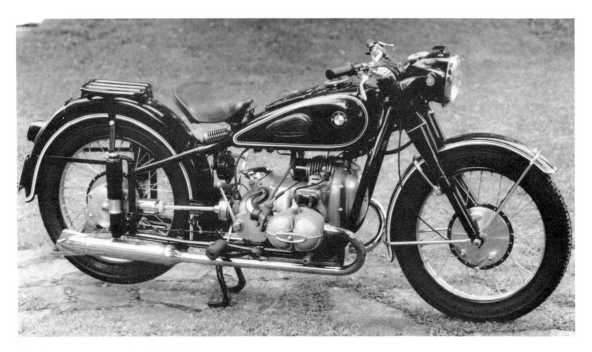

The first post-war twin, the R50/2.

kept so that pre-war crankcases could be utilised. Just where the crankcases came from is not explained! It seems unlikely that the number needed could have been hidden in a barn and a more likely explanation is that the moulds survived and surplus aeroplane aluminium was utilised.

Another cost-cutting exercise was the substitution of needle-roller rocker bearings by more simple and cheaper plain bushes. The valve springs were changed from hairpin to coil and, to create more room for the rider's feet, the carburettors (now made exclusively by Bing and having a 22mm choke) were inclined inwards and sloped downwards. Although the carbs still vented into the space above the gearbox, a proper air filter had not yet been introduced. The smooth rocker covers with oil filters in the top were replaced by the twin type as used on the R75, suggesting, perhaps, that they had salvaged the moulds from the *Wehrmacht* machine.

There was also a link between the new cylinder heads of the R51/2 and those of the R75. The lubrication to the rocker area was now accomplished by way of hollow tappets and pushrods, which acted as oilways. There was obviously merit in the idea, for it lasted until the arrival of the /5 models in 1969.

Some pre-war sophistication survived. The engine was the last to use twin camshafts, and the tank-top toolbox introduced in 1935 was retained – it has survived, in one form or another, until recently, on police bikes. Ignition was still by coil with a dynamo mounted above the crankcase but the output was now 75w, which was the most powerful yet on a BMW motorcycle. More deeply valanced mudguards than those used previously were also fitted.

The cycle parts were much the same as the R51 except for the previously mentioned mudguards but, as on the R24, the handlebar levers were no longer inverted. The frame

Pre-war orgins are obvious in this 1950 R51/2.

had been strengthened with an extra brace welded in place at the top of the twin front down-tubes, and an extra support running from the cross brace to the rear of the top tube.

Although the 24PS power output of the engine was the same as that of the original R51 and the top speed was still in the region of 87mph (140kph), weight had taken its familiar upswing and was now 407lb (185kg). In spite of its high price, the motorcycling world was hungry for such a machine and 5,000 examples were made during its short production run. Soon, a new R51 would appear and the power unit would form the basis of all BMW boxers until the end of the Earles-forked machines in 1969.

PRODUCTION RACING

As BMW interest in Grand Prix racing diminished so the efforts of those who made and sold BMWs turned towards production racing. Great Britain became the focal point of this interest and a small West London dealer, MLG, who had been selling and repairing BMWs since 1949, took the first tentative step into production racing by entering a stock R69 in the 1958 Thruxton 500-mile race. Competitors fell about laughing when they realised that the bike really was an over-the-counter example. Most of the serious competitors knew different and the term 'stock' was given a rather liberal interpretation. In spite of this

Racing a road-going sidecar outfit is never easy, particularly when the sidecar is on the 'wrong' side. Keith Sanders was the author's passenger when the R60/Steib outfit was raced at Silverstone.

the BMW, ridden by John Lewis and Peter James, came third. The competition was faster and handled better, but the BMW kept going.

A year later MLG were back at Thruxton, armed with a more competitive machine and extra know-how from the factory. John Lewis was now partnered by Peter Darvill and the black BMW whispered its way to a win that left the opposition gasping. A second machine crashed out of the race when Phil Read, who would one day be world champion, got into trouble on the back of the circuit. Perhaps the greatest win of all for the MLG BMW was in Barcelona. They turned up with bikes that were really too big and heavy for the twisting Spanish circuit, yet riders Peter Darvill and Bruce Daniels beat the opposition out of sight.

In 1960 the Lewis/Darvill partnership won again at Thruxton. Soon after, the win was repeated at Silverstone in the 1,000 Kilometre race, whilst another emphatic win in Spain in the Barcelona Twenty-Four Hour race on a tortuous 1¼ mile circuit, again tested the stamina of the machine and its riders to the full. This time Darvill was partnered by Norman Price.

Winning showed the world just how good the BMW was and did sales no harm at all. Until MLG started winning long-distance production races, the Munich bikes were seen as rather staid gentlemen's tourers. Now the motorcycling public looked at the machines with new respect. MLG had proved that the BMW was more than just an expensive toy and they retired from production machine racing.

A classic – the 1960–1969 R69S.

MLG's sporting involvement also extended to record breaking and, in 1961, using an R69S that had the 'encouragement' of the factory, they planned an assault on the world 24-hour record at Monthléry. Velocette had recently become the first manufacturer to average 100mph (160kph) for twenty-four hours, taking the record from a French-prepared BMW.

Two attempts were needed for the MLG BMW to snatch the record. Tragically, the first try resulted in one of the teamsters, Peter Lawford, being killed when he rode his bike over the outer rim of the banked track. It was a while before MLG had the heart to return, but return they did and a team of British riders scooped the world 24-hour record at an average speed of over 109mph (175kph) including stops. For good measure they also added the 1-hour and 12-hour

record. The riders were Sid Mizen, Ellis Boyce, George Catlin and John Holder, all accomplished racers. Coincidentally, this record too was to stand for fourteen years before Kawasaki claimed it. This time, though, there was no war to extend the time lapse.

REBIRTH

By 1951 the BMW factory was working to full capacity. Motorcycle production had risen from 9,450 in 1949 to 17,100 the following year, with the 1951–1952 figures reaching 25,000. BMW had not lost sight of their dual role as both car and motorcycle manufacturers and, with the motorcycle division successful, were able to look at a return to car manufacture. In this case it was not as straight-forward (one hesitates to use the word 'easy' to describe the efforts of BMW in the immediate post-war years), for car production had been in Eisenach, now located east of the Iron Curtain. The factory had been taken into what was called 'national ownership' by the Soviet Union, and, in addition to the continued production of the R35 motorcycle, they also made BMW cars, using the same pre-war designs. Initially the 321 and 327 were made, but, as time went on, modifications were introduced and the factory even dabbled in Formula 2 racing. In 1955 the Eisenach works became Automobilewerk Eisenach and the BMW connection was broken.

Car production was once again centred on Munich. In spite of the difficulties a BMW car was prepared for the 1951 Frankfurt Show; the hand-made, two-litre six-cylinder 501 was unveiled. Customers clamoured for what was one of the most beautiful cars at the show, but salesmen on the stand could only take orders, as no delivery date could be given. The 501 was, like the recently introduced motorcycles, not exactly a new model, rather a modified version of the tremendously successful pre-war saloons. The success of the BMW car in the 1930s was both sporting and financial, and their model 328 two-seater sports car was on a par with MG when it came to looks and superior performance. Sadly, that delightful little two-seater never reappeared, for the company decided that their car future lay in the luxury market, a similar philosophy to that applied to the motorcycle division.

Luxury cars were available only to a limited number of customers in austere post-war Europe and designs were considered for a new 'baby' car. One such design was a small saloon not unlike the Volkswagen but with more handsome lines. It was almost a scaled-down version of the 501. For whatever reason it was not adopted and, in 1954, the company threw in its lot with the current clamour for

bubble cars. The Italian Iso company were already manufacturing a well-designed one and BMW decided to make it under licence, calling it the Isetta and substituting its two-stroke engine with a modified single-cylinder engine as was used in the R25.

Bubble car aptly described the Isetta, for that is what it looked like. It was a three-wheeler with a single wheel at the rear (a twin-wheel version was also made but did not conform to British tax regulations) and two front wheels. A steering-wheel was cranked to (more or less) move out of the way when the front door was opened. The Isetta would take two people but little more. A 250cc engine was used, with the option of one increased to 300cc, and an electric starter was added. Drive was to the rear wheel and few owners escaped the attention of jokers who could easily lift the wheel off the ground at the moment of departure.

Whether the adoption of the Isetta was a good move in the long run is debatable, but 150,000 were sold between 1954 and 1963 and much publicity was generated. Remember that, in 1954, the public was beginning to realise that it was possible to broaden horizons in a way undreamed of by those who had lived in the 1930s. A really cheap practical car was not yet on the market and the BMW Isetta seemed to bridge the gap nicely. It was originally imported into Great Britain from Germany but before long an English manufacturer, Isetta of Great Britain, contracted to build it under licence and the BMW badge on the front was dropped.

To have a ride in one was an unforgettable experience. Isettas were noisy, vibratory and not very fast. Safety was not something that exercised designers' minds too much in those days and no-one considered how the occupants would be released if the Isetta ran into the back of another vehicle, for it had only a front opening door. In fairness, the author has no recollection of anything really untoward happening to Isetta owners except, perhaps, that they took rather longer to arrive than expected. Motorcycle owners tended to look down on them as, perhaps, threats to their way of life. People seeking a 'proper' car accepted them, at best, as tolerable until they could afford something better.

Of all the models sold in Great Britain, few have survived. History has not been kind to designs that proved to be no more than a passing fad, but many British motorists were attracted by the charms of the Isetta and an Isetta Club still survives (*see* Useful Addresses, page 172).

Possibly the most interesting version was a 600cc four-wheeler designed and produced by BMW and incorporating three doors. It was quite an attractive little car and, given a bit of luck, it just might have caught the public's imagination. Unfortunately for BMW a man called Issigonis came along and designed the Mini, which consigned the Isetta, along with the similar Heinkel – the 'different' Messerschmitt (possibly the nearest thing to a motorcycle with a roof) – and sidecar outfits, to the enthusiasts. They were no longer considered a cheap, economical way of transporting a family.

FULL-SCALE PRODUCTION

With demand for BMW motorcycles high, the company seized the opportunity to continue what they had begun back in 1923: a process of evolution, incorporating new ideas into existing proven ones. This time their attention was turned to the engines and a new generation was designed. They were to remain on the whole unchanged until 1969.

Two new models, the R51/3 and the R67, were introduced in 1951. Naturally the tried and tested boxer layout was retained. It was universally accepted as being one of the best motorcycle engines ever made and, notwith-

standing the occasional complaints about vulnerable cylinders sticking out of the side, many well-heeled motorcyclists were still inclined to choose a BMW.

The whole engine unit was tidied up in time for 1951: the twin chain-driven camshaft, first offered on a production BMW in 1938, was abandoned for a single spur-gear driven camshaft, still operating pushrods that ran from the top of the crankshaft. There were now no chains in the motor, and the oil-pump and camshaft were gear driven.

Electrical generation was still by dynamo, but this had been moved from the top of the engine to a dry home inside the front engine cover and was bolted to the end of the crankshaft. It produced an almost unheard of 160 watts, a far cry from the 60-watt units that were still considered adequate for some machines. In consequence the rider was treated to extremely good lights, a 35/35 watts headlight being supplemented for the first time by a stop lamp fitted as standard. A touch of luxury came in the shape of a neutral indicator lamp in the headlamp shell. It was considered rather 'sissy' by some, but is the norm today.

Coil ignition was abolished and a Norris magneto provided the sparks, removing the need for a battery to provide the initial spark, although one was still supplied. The magneto was secured to the end of the crankcase, onto the removable cover which isolated the timing gears from the electrics, with the camshaft operating the points. Bob-weights gave automatic advance and retard, and adjustment could be made by pivoting the unit. Marks on the flywheel indicated not only at which point the spark was fully retarded and advanced, but also when the pistons were at top dead centre (for tappet adjustment). A cast front cover was bolted over the whole electrical system, keeping dynamo, points and generator clean and dry no matter what the weather.

Franz Marek's superb 1953 R51/3.

The cylinder base now joined the heads in having a four-stud fixing. The fifth stud secured a clamp which kept the pushrod rubbers tights in their recesses. The pushrod rubbers were now just a push fit. Many years previously, 'H' section connecting-rods had joined the pistons to the crankshaft; these connecting-rods now became 'I' type. Carburettors were still 22mm Bings (24mm on the 60), but a very good air filter was now mounted above the gearbox. New rocker covers immediately identified the new machines – six fin covers being used on both.

Despite all the changes, the power output of the new R51/3 remained the same (at 24PS), as did the top speed. The weight had gone up yet again and now stood at 418lb (190kg), some 22lb (10kg) more than the previous model. Changes to the cycle parts

were minimal and even the silencers were initially identical to those used on the R51/2. By 1952 even this had changed, for the new 'torpedo' silencer was used on all models. Again, it is hard to escape the feeling that old stock was being used up; fin type silencers had been a feature of BMW motorcycles since 1935 so the factory could hardly be accused of rushing things.

One welcome throw-back to pre-war years was the steering-lock. BMW was almost alone in deeming such an item necessary and the lock used in the early 1950s was a long brass billet that the rider inserted in holes positioned in the front forks and steering yoke. It was very robust but meant that a place had to be found for a rather large lump of brass when the lock was not in use. Fuel tank capacity was increased to 3.75 gallons (17 litres) and the tank-top toolbox was

A clean climb of Darracott for the R51/3 in the 1962 Lands End Trial.

retained. Fuel consumption of the R51/3 and the R67 was, at about 62mpg, the same.

Slightly more power (26PS at 5,500rpm) was available on the 600 but only another 3mph on the top speed. The weight was just 4.5lb (2kg) more than the 500. Both bore and stroke were increased and a lower compression ratio (5.6:1 compared to 6.3:1 on the 500) gave a soft, tractable, 'torquey' engine that was ideal for sidecar work.

The production run of the R51/3 and R67 – soon to become the R67/2 – continued virtu-ally unchanged until 1954 but detail modifications were made. Perhaps the most noteworthy of these was the introduction of twin leading shoe front-brakes in 1952. They immediately gave the machine a degree of stopping power rare in a production motor-cycle. A year later the front forks were improved to introduce two-way damping, a move which coincided with the introduction of front-fork gaiters on all models. At the same time the interchangeable wheels sported full-width hubs and light alloy rims.

Geoff Arkle cruises up Hustyn on his R51 in the Lands End Trial.

The maximum power of the 600 was boosted to 28PS, achieved with just 100 extra rpm.

In 1955, a new BMW series was announced; the R67 was modified, however, and sold for another two years as a complete sidecar outfit, with all three wheels being interchangeable. It was clear that the Steib TR500 sidecar owed its origins to the *Wehrmacht* R75 – as did much of the new engine. Also fitted was a hydraulic sidecar brake, linked to the rear one. The idea was superb but it required patience to keep it properly adjusted. The author had a memo-rable experience in Esher High Street when the hydraulics to the sidecar took control and locked the sidecar wheel, sending the whole outfit pirouetting in front of startled spectators.

In 1953 BMW sold its 100,000th motor-cycle since the end of the war, but analysts had begun to realise that the heyday of the motorcycle was nearing an end. There were still a few years to go, but even at this stage the heavier BMWs were not selling as well as they had done in the past.

7 The 100mph Motorcycle

A year after the new 500 and 600cc machines appeared on the market, BMW announced the arrival of an immediate teaser: the R68. Introduced by the company as 'The 100mph motorcycle', it delighted BMW fans the world over. It came in two guises, one for road and one for cross-country use, with the track version sporting an upswept siamesed exhaust system, wider handlebars, a separate pillion pad and a raised rear number-plate. Conventional exhaust pipes were used on the road version but the pipe was slightly larger than that on the touring machines, as many an owner found to his cost when trying to fit R67 silencers onto an R68.

The cross-country machines used a single-fin type silencer, with the twin pipes crossing over the top of the engine and exiting on the right. It made a lovely, flat, muted sound. The new torpedo silencers were used on the R68 but had a slightly greater diameter to fit the larger exhaust pipe. Those silencers were to characterise the remainder of the production run until 1969. A finned ring retained the exhaust to the head – a system that is used right to the present day – which is no easier to undo without a special spanner now than it was then.

Dimensions of the new R68 were identical to those of its softer stablemate, the R67, with the same bore and stroke and electrics. Where it differed was in the engine internals. The compression ratio was raised to 7.7:1 and larger 26mm Bing carburettors were fitted. Internally the most interesting change was to the rear main bearing which

was now fully floating, an arrangement which allowed for a little crankshaft flexibility. A reinforced crankshaft housing was also used.

The power output received a considerable boost from the more efficient engine, and 35PS was claimed at 7,000rpm. It was the greatest power and highest revs yet seen on a road-going BMW and gave the bike a top speed of 100mph (160kph). By the standards of the day there were machines around, notably the Vincent and the more sporting British twins, that could do better than this, but it was the way that the R68 achieved it which made it such a pleasing bike to ride.

As an aid to engine flexibility, an additional ignition control fitted on the handlebars gave the rider the option of retarding the ignition for cold starting (the R68 had three degrees more advance with the advance and retard bob-weights at rest than the touring machines). It also proved useful for coping with some of the inferior fuels around, again by retarding the ignition a little.

Deeply valanced mudguards had become a feature of the touring machines but on the sports model less ample ones were considered appropriate. A chrome-plated grab rail was an interesting addition to the specification, doubtless proving useful when hauling the off-road version out of deep mud. Narrower sports handlebars were fitted to the machine and adjustable pillion rests were extolled as a virtue. The lugs for those rests were a part of the touring models – not surprisingly, as it used the same frame – but the rider would have had to pay extra if he wanted the footrests as well! The recently introduced twin leading shoe front-brake was a standard fitting.

One easy way to identify BMW sports models after the introduction of the R68 was by their rocker covers which had just two fins. They somehow came to represent the essence of the sporting BMW and the design survived right up to the introduction of the /7 series in 1976.

Small numbers of the R68 in ISDT trim, which was how the bike with the upswept pipes was defined, were used in these gruelling trials events by amateur owners. For a machine that was really all wrong for the type of going encountered it did well. One British owner, Geoff Arkle, took his over-the-counter R68, which weighed in at 425lb (193kg), through the 1954 ISDT in Wales and finished the course. It was quite an achievement for a rider with no works support.

When the R68 was replaced by the new generation R69 in 1955, just 1,452 examples had been made. The price was rather more than that of the touring models and not many were brought into Great Britain. As is so often the case, very few are seen around nowadays but there is no shortage of prospective customers should one come on the market.

A very good example of the 1953 R25/3.

THRIVING SINGLES

By 1953 the BMW single was clearly lagging behind its twin-cylinder counterparts. Development had been concentrated on the twins and the old R25 was in need of a facelift. This came with the introduction of the R25/3. A /2 had briefly appeared which was little changed from the R25, whereas the /3 was given a comprehensive redesign and had, if anything, more to show for it than the twins. The engine was boosted by a mere 1PS to 13PS but it was enough to give the

machine an enormous performance boost, increasing its top speed by 14mph (24kph) to 73mph (119kph). In 1953, 70mph (113kph) was considered a fair top speed for the average 350, so the BMW single could be considered to have above-average performance for its class. There was no problem reaching the speed claimed.

Changes to the engine were numerous. Carburettor size was increased to 24mm, the same size as that on the R67. The air intake was by way of a convoluted passage scooping cool air through a filter at the front of the fuel tank and carrying it by a tube to the carburettor. Bore and stroke dimensions remained the same but the compression ratio had increased to 7:1. An improved cylinder

Things did not always go according to plan. The author's only failure (on Simms) in the 1962 Exeter Trial and a photographer just has to be there. The machine was an MLG-loaned ex-ISDT R25 special.

head and wider finning gave the engine a more substantial look which, with the improved breathing, enabled the new 250 to use a much higher rear-drive for the same top-gear ratio, thereby assisting top speed. All the improvements to the carburation clearly made for a very efficient engine: fuel consumption was claimed to be 98mpg, and even with a sidecar attached the claim was for 77mpg.

Front forks were now two-way hydraulically damped whilst both front and rear units had longer travel. Full width hubs were a

part of the new R25/3 but the twin leading shoe front-brake used on the twins was not considered necessary. As the machine was also intended for sidecar use a number of combination owners might have disagreed.

Some features that would also appear on the soon-to-be-launched Earles-fork models were introduced on the single. The toolbox was lockable and recessed into the left side of the fuel tank. The steering-lock was now set into the steering-head, which saved the rider from the encumbrance of the brass billet when the lock was not in use. As on the bigger bikes, a steering-damper was standard (mainly for sidecar use) and comfort was improved by the use of the Pagusa adjustable swing saddle.

Sidecar enthusiasts could buy a complete BMW outfit with, as usual, fully interchangeable wheels. Sidecar lugs were standard. The sidecar used on the 250 was the model Steib LS200, a handsome chair which soon found its way to bigger machines. No less than 47,700 R25/3s were made during the machine's three-year run.

Moving on to 1955 we come to the introduction of the R26. This bike joined the twins in heralding a new era of motorcycling. The comfort and style of the R26 were acclaimed by all who rode it. The same cannot be said, unfortunately, about the gearbox, which was clunky even by BMW standards. Performance, however, was outstanding with top speed just on 80mph (128kph). This was achieved by boosting the compression ratio to 7.5:1 and increasing the carburettor induction size yet again, to 26mm (the same as on the R69). Although the literature of the day says that the bike had generator and magneto ignition, it still utilised a coil, and a battery was needed to assist in starting. Power output was now 15PS at 6,400rpm.

However, it was not the engine that made the new BMWs different: it was the chassis. The front forks were devised by a British designer, Ernie Earles, and introduced a degree of comfort that was almost unknown on a motorcycle. These forks features short travel suspension units, similar in size to those used on the rear, and the suspension pivoted on taper roller bearings at the bottom of the rear fork tube. They took a little getting used to, for, instead of the forks dipping when the brakes were applied, the front end rose. Touring riders found it suited the machine admirably. It took a little more adjusting to in competitive arenas although Gilera were using forks with the same design at that time. Similar forks were used by

Douglas and (in prototype form) by Ariel but the idea never really appealed to mainline motorcycle manufacturers: old traditions die hard.

Still used was a twin down-tube cradle frame with the bracing across the front that was introduced on the R51/2. Smaller wheels were announced for all models with the arrival of the 'Earles-fork BMWs' as they soon became known. Wheels were now interchangeable, 18in front and rear.

A second major change came with the rear-suspension. It was of the increasingly popular swinging-arm type but, because the frame was attached not at the top of the units but half way down, there was scope for considerably more suspension movement. The frame now formed a loop at the rear with the suspension casing welded to the back of the loop, having an extra attachment point on the rear mud-guard. The substantial rear sub-frame enclosed the cardan shaft – a gearbox end universal coupling having replaced the bonded rubber connection – in its right leg. Suspension movement front and rear was incredible by the standards of the day and the new bikes were a magic carpet ride compared with previous models. A bonus for sidecar riders was that the new front forks had adjustable lead, the rear pivot having a second position more suited to sidecar use.

It was inevitable that all the sophistication introduced on the new model should carry a weight penalty and the new 250 turned the scales at 348lb (158kg), some 17.6lb (8kg) more than its predecessor. This contributed to a reduction in fuel consumption too, and the R26 was now stated to return 86mpg. Strangely, the claim for the amount of fuel used when a sidecar was attached remained the same.

Over 30,000 examples were sold during the five years the bike was in the catalogue and in that time it remained virtually unchanged.

In 1960 the R26 was superseded by the

This much-modified German-owned R26 is a regular visitor to the Pre-65 Talmag Trial, held in Surrey, England, in January.

R27 and followed the same pattern. Although BMW 250s had earned a faithful following, there were constant complaints that the engine, which differed from other singles in that its crankshaft ran longitudinally rather than across the frame, vibrated too much. In an effort to absorb rather than cure, the R27's engine was rubber-mounted. Those who owned the R27 swore that they no longer felt any vibration. Those who tested it were not so sure.

Unlike the twins, the post-war singles used a chain to drive the camshaft. On the R27, a self-adjusting tensioner was added in an additional effort to curtail vibration, and for the same reason the compression ratio was increased yet again to 8.2:1, and the motor now produced 18PS. Top speed was only marginally better at 81mph (130kph). The machine never really set the sales charts alight, with only just over 15,000 sold worldwide during the bike's seven-year production run. It was to be the last single made by BMW – at least until the F650 Funduro arrived.

THE BEST BMW YET?

Were R50/60/69 series BMWs the best motorcycles produced by the company? It is the author's view that they were. They introduced sophistication and comfort that had never been seen before on a motorcycle. In addition they were incredibly reliable, did not leak oil and achieved a degree of silence, both mechanical and from the exhaust, that was unsurpassed. Oh and yes, they were expensive, too.

First to be introduced were the R26, R50 and R69 in 1955 (although the models had been known of a year earlier). It was the suspension that provided the major changes for, as on the R26, the new chassis and suspension system announced that BMW were still serious about motorcycling despite a less buoyant market. Changes to the engines were minor but significant. Previously the single-plate clutch was controlled by a series of springs: an arrangement that required the agility of a slip fielder when dismantling the assembly with the engine in the frame. A diaphragm spring was now given the task.

On the R50, which took over from the R51/3, a 24mm Bing carburettor replaced the 22mm version and the compression ratio was increased by half a point to 6.8:1. Power output was up from 22 to 24PS which must have just about compensated for the extra 11lb (5kg) that the machine carried, for the top speed of 87mph (140kph) was the same as that of the R51/3.

It was a slightly different story with the R68's replacement, the R69. In this case the carburettor size remained the same, as did the power output, but top speed was up by 3mph (5kph) whilst the maximum revs were down by 200 to 6,800.

The diaphragm clutch was now standard on all models and would be for the future. So too was a new three-shaft gearbox. For all the machine's virtues, BMW riders had long complained that changing gear was ponderous and – unless the engine/gearbox speed relationship was just right – noisy. There were numerous attempts to overcome the problem of gear changing with an engine speed clutch but a solution was a long way ahead yet. On the other hand 'real' BMW owners prided themselves in being able to accomplish silent gearchanges with or without the use of the clutch. Let no one say that it could be achieved without skill and practice, though.

All the new models used interchangeable 18in wheels and the twins shared a common chassis. A small but much appreciated feature of all the new models was a large, elegant rear light. Riders soon found that the shell was also a useful storage place for a spare bulb but it was more often than not *kaput* when the need came. By the standards of the day BMW engines did not vibrate, indeed they had always been famous for their smoothness, but it was perhaps stretching charity too much to expect a bulb to survive for years at the extreme end of a motorcycle!

Just one year later came the final piece in this particular jigsaw when the R67 became the R60. It now had a power output of 28PS, an increase of 2PS, and a compression ratio bumped up from a nice soft 5.6:1 to a hardly less soft 6.5:1. There was no change in performance, and for a 590cc engine a top speed of only 90mph (145kph) was undoubtedly on the tame side. Performance seekers could opt for the sporting R69. Only just over 3,500 R60s and under 1,300 R69s were sold between 1956 and 1960 and sales figures such as these were part of the reason why, in 1959, the company was in dire financial trouble.

IN THE RED

BMW entered the 1950s with high hopes. BMW motorcycles, the linchpin of the company, were acclaimed the world over, and the BMW sports cars, hand-made delights that could compete with the best, had resumed production. The BMW Isetta was a fine 'bread and butter' product (but rather short on the jam) and in 1956 the thriving aero-engine division was awarded a contract to build 400 Pratt & Whitney jet engines. In spite of the fact that it was many years since a dividend had been paid, all the signs of a successful and thriving company were there to be seen.

Yet, in 1958, the bubble burst. In 1958 the reserves were seriously depleted and a year later they were all gone. There was increasing talk of mergers and takeovers and by 1959 the company was in the red. At a general meeting in Munich there appeared to be no way out for the company and it looked as if it would have to be sold.

That such a thing could happen was unbelievable, even to Germans uninvolved with the company. Mercedes were on the verge of taking the company over, but not everyone had given up hope and a small group of shareholders demanded that the announcement of BMW's dissolution be deferred. Maybe they knew that a saviour was at hand.

Dr Herbert Quandt was that saviour, and his interest in the company caused the big banks to regain confidence in it. MAN, the equally well-known manufacturer, famous for its heavy vehicles, came galloping to the rescue with a promise to cover BMW's debts.

Dr Herbert Quandt

Quandt was not an engineer, neither was he known as a motorcycle enthusiast. Yet it was he, amongst all others, who kept the name BMW alive when, in 1959, the company was on the verge of collapse. He was a banker of some repute and gave BMW his backing when the company was about to sign a deal with their great rival, Mercedes-Benz.

His interest caused others to regain confidence in BMW and, with MAN, the heavy vehicle maker, buying the aero-engine sector off the company and promising to cover their debts, BMW were able to start the long process of rebuilding.

They also purchased the aero-engine division, based at Allach, and the BMW interest in aeroplanes was severed.

Whilst all this had been going on a new car was on the drawing board. Known as the BMW 700 it was to be a final attempt by BMW to enter the small (if not economy) car market, and the engine chosen was an enlarged version of the 600cc boxer used in the motorcycles. With the injection of capital from the big banks it was possible to put the car into volume production and the BMW 700 was an immediate success. It was pretty basic by BMW standards, looking not unlike the then-popular Triumph Herald (but without that car's incredibly small turning circle), but it did bring in the cash and enabled the company to set their sights on doing what they do best: up-market quality vehicles. (Probably the most attractive of those was the cabriolet, which, using the 40PS engine, had a top speed of 83mph (133kph). If any have survived, they are kept very well hidden.)

No one who understood the philosophy of the BMW company could imagine that the 700 was anything more than a stop-gap whilst they regained their equilibrium. This balance was achieved at the 1961 Frankfurt Show when the first new BMW 1500 was shown. No longer was it profitable to build 'hand-made' motors for discerning gentlemen; the new 1500 – to be followed by larger versions – immediately hit a target that BMW have been peppering ever since, that of the quality but affordable (just!) sports saloon.

Within two years the shareholders were paid their first dividend since before the war and the future now depended on the sales of motor cars. Motorcycles were no longer the most important part of BMW, and in future they would be made as an act of faith rather than as a profit-making exercise.

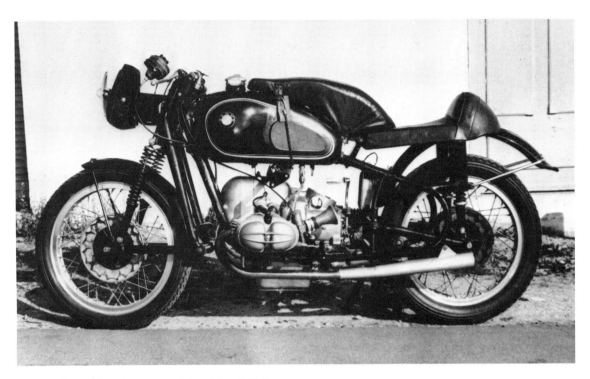

The MLG world 24-hour record-breaking R69S.

MORE FINE TUNING

Production of the Earles-type motorcycles continued throughout the financial problems of the late 1950s. The designers and engineers, with admirable single-mindedness, managed to put the financial wrangling off their minds and continued to look at ways of improving the product.

In 1960, what was to be the final development of the traditional boxer engine was announced. As always the changes were undramatic, merely fine-tuning all the models to improve both comfort and performance. A new 500 was announced, the R50S, sharing the same twin-finned rocker covers with the new R69S. Performance was boosted from the 30PS of the R50/2 (which was in turn 2PS greater than its predecessor) and the carburettors were increased by the

now almost obligatory 2mm to 26mm. Although these were of the same choke size as the discontinued R69, they were of a different designation. Performance was increased by the use of larger diameter exhaust valves and top speed was now 100mph (160kph).

In most other respects the engine was similar to that of the R50/2, but a vibration damper was fitted to the end of the crankshaft. In achieving its top speed the high performance 490cc engine reached the highest revs yet for a road-going BMW, developing 35PS at 7,650rpm. Both 500s had a stronger crankshaft and a more robust 20mm taper on the dynamo, whilst the S model had a considerably improved rotary disc crankcase vent.

Top speed of the R69S was 109mph (175kph), just over 6mph (10kph) faster than

Waterloo was an appropriate name for this Exeter Trial hill. The machine is the author's faithful R60 with a right-hand Steib, the year is 1966.

the much-loved R69. It, too, had the crank-shaft damper, which was a steel disc mounted on a vulcanised ring. Surprisingly the S did not have larger-sized carburettors and shared the same 26mm choke size with the R50S. A different model was used, though.

Another small addition was a hydraulic steering damper in place of the friction one used on other models. Those who attached sidecars to the R69S, and many did, soon

found that the new damper was no use at all for a three-wheeler.

A new air filter casing helped enthusiasts to identify the new model. The pronounced bulge at the front where the crankshaft damper went was a help, too! There was no hump on the 500. The dualseat was now a standard fitting but it was still possible to order the Pagusa swing saddle instead – although a rubber block had replaced the adjustable spring. Right-hand sidecar lugs

Racing a sidecar outfit at Silverstone in the 'old days' (1966) included sharing the track with Morgans, which were either very fast or pointing the wrong way. Passenger Keith Sanders, the author the driver.

were standard on all models, and for a short time, in 1960, models were imported with lugs on the left instead.

There was one incredible departure from tradition, yet it was accepted with barely a murmur. For the first time it was possible, in the early 1960s, to buy a BMW in a colour other than black, for an option white with black pinstriping became available. It was an immediate success amongst the younger customers but older BMW riders tended to be a little dismissive about the whole concept. In addition to white, BMW listed a variety of colours to special order (for an extra £10) but it is a comment on the conservatism of British BMW owners that, if any were ordered, they were kept under wraps. The author has no recollection of ever seeing a factory-prepared machine in any colour other than black or white during this period – excepting, of course, the bilious green used by the German police.

Racing success and the proven quality of the BMW twins boosted sales in Great Britain. From 1960 to 1967, 8,000 R60s and 11,319 R69Ss were made and sold worldwide, small numbers by the standards of the Japanese, who had by now arrived to give motorcycling a much needed boost, but enough to keep the production lines rolling. Sadly, the R50S never caught on. Seekers after a performance BMW chose the bigger machine and only 1,634 R50Ss were sold during the bike's three-year production life. By 1967 BMW had produced their 250,000th motorcycle since the end of World War II.

One last change was introduced in 1967. Almost as a prelude to the next generation of BMWs, which would be announced two years later, the company produced the R60US and the R69US models (a designation that caused a little smile among riders of rival marques, although US meant United States), scrapping the Earles-type front-suspension and returning to telescopic forks. They were almost exactly the same as those used on the /5 series of BMWs, whose introduction in 1969 coincided with a move to new

Hustyn in the 1964 Lands End Trial. Photographer and rider finished up on the ground together.

premises at Spandau, West Berlin, which, in pre-war days, had housed a BMW production line.

Production of the boxers continued to drop and now reached a low of 6,000 units a year. At the same time, the annual production of cars had risen by thirty-three per cent with almost 145,000 made in 1969. The stage was set for a whole new concept of the boxer-engine machines, and for public acceptance at a level that had not previously been considered possible.

8 A BMW Revolution

Such a title might seem a little over-the-top for a company that had always believed in evolution, but the arrival in 1969 of the /5 series BMW was undoubtedly the most dramatic and fundamental change to the machines since their introduction in 1923.

Three new models were announced, the R50/5, the R60/5 and the R75/5, with capacities almost corresponding to the model numbers. All featured entirely new engines and BMW had, literally, stood the whole boxer concept on its head: the camshaft which had long sat *above* the crankshaft was now situated *below* the crankshaft. The pushrods, formerly in tubes above the cylinders, were now banished to similar tubes out of sight below the engine.

The most fundamental change was to the lubrication system: the old low pressure oil circulation was abandoned (and with it the thrower plates) and a high pressure system was introduced, with circulation by Eaton

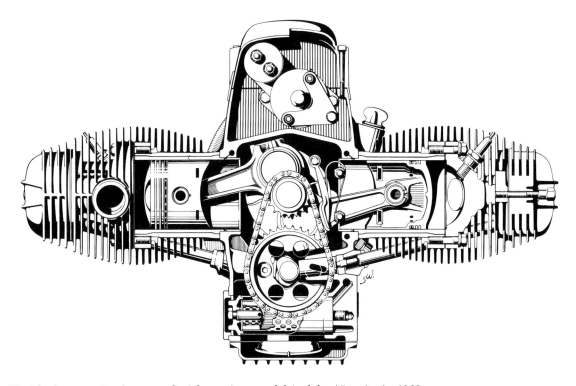

Upside-down engine (compared with previous models) of the /5 series in 1969.

A new era for BMW, the /5 series featuring electric starter and high pressure oiling system. Gone were the Earles-type front forks and interchangeable wheels.

pump. Such an arrangement had many virtues, not the least being that it was more suitable for modern multi-grade oils. However, it was less forgiving if the owner chose to work the engine hard before the oil had had time to circulate.

Tradition dies hard, though, and much of the early thinking remained. Pushrod-operated overhead-valve operation was retained rather than the more efficient but more complicated overhead camshaft arrangement. The handsome twin-fin rocker covers survived, at least for a few more years. Bing carburettors were still used; the shape had changed but activation on the two

smaller models was still by slide. On the R75, Bing introduced constant depression carburettors, also known as the vacuum type. Initially the reliability was suspect, but before long the problem was solved and this type of carburettor is still used on the larger twins.

Such changes would have been considered quite enough but BMW did something that they had never done before: they changed everything. The /5s were totally different machines to the Earles-type models; there was no area that remained untouched. Ever since the day the first boxer was made the company had considered that six volts was

Riding the Funduro in France.

Lanzarote and the R1100RS.

Sani Pass, Lesotho, with the author on the R100GS.

ABS as fitted to the rear wheel.

Bright colours on the R1100GS.

Cutaway illustration of the R100GS.

Touring on the R100RT.

*The author on his 1964
R60/2.*

Hans-Otto Butenuth's 500cc Rennsport in the Isle of Man.

Two views of the R1100RT. In the studio (right) and out on the open road (below).

The BMW R100RT Classic.

BMW 100R Boxer Classic.

Sectioned model of the K75.

The R1100RT – state of the art BMW motorcycling.

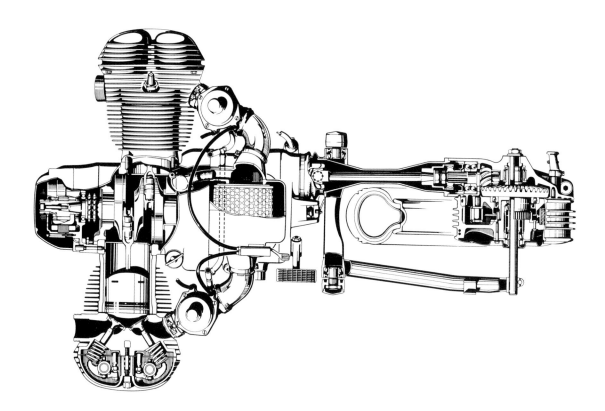

Engine layout of the R75/5.

adequate. Now, not only did they incorporate the twelve-volt system that had appeared on the later R69US but also an electric starter, mounted under a cover on top of the engine. On the 500 it was optional, but the 600 and 750 had this unheard-of luxury as a standard fitting. Additionally, there were now flashing indicators – those had been available for the previous ten years but were something of an afterthought, with single lights on the ends of the handlebars. Few riders bothered, for the six-volt system and comparatively low output dynamo did not really produce enough power for adequate illumination. On the new machines the indicators were positioned front and rear and were superb.

It follows that the headlight, too, benefited from twelve-volt bulbs, and the power for all

this came from a generator producing no less than 200 watts. It was far higher than anything previously seen on a production motorcycle. Initially a 24 amp-hour battery was specified, but the power needed to turn over a twin-cylinder engine was considerable and it was soon increased to 28 amp-hour. It was still barely enough. Perhaps in recognition of this, the kickstarter remained in position. When it was finally abandoned some years later it remained for a while as an expensive, but much sought-after, optional extra.

Initially a four-speed gearbox was specified, but the introduction of a five-speed version was not far away. A single plate clutch operated by a diaphragm continued to carry the power from engine to gearbox, but was now listed as having a disc spring.

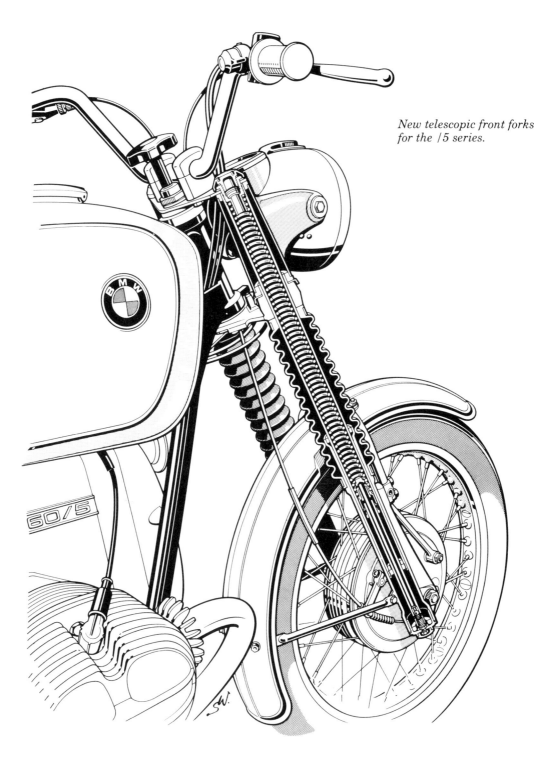

New telescopic front forks for the /5 series.

The front forks introduced two years earlier were complemented by a suspension that was now similar to that of most other sports machines: that is, swinging-arm with the attachment points bolted to the top and bottom of the twin adjustable suspension units. A twin cradle frame using an oval tube was retained but the rear sub-frame was now bolted up. It looked rather unsubstantial, but twenty years' use has proved otherwise.

For the first time, though, sidecars fitted to the BMW range were no longer authorised (a particularly German way of saying that if owners did fit one the warranty would be invalid). In fact the company positively discouraged it. Owners, of course, thought they knew better. Anxious to utilise the extra power of the 750 engine, they found that there were ways of overcoming the weak rear-end. They worked, too, most of the time!

Interchangeable wheels had long been a feature of the BMWs but increasing the front wheel size to 19in and retaining an 18in rear one put a stop to all that. Those who liked to carry a spare inner tube now had to carry two. BMW did remain one of the few manufacturers to supply a hand pump as standard; and the toolkit, which had always been superb, still included tyre levers. Drum brakes front and rear were standard, with the well established twin leading shoe front-brake still considered adequate.

A larger fuel tank, similar in shape to that marketed as an extra for many years by George Meier, now accepted just under 5 gallons (22 litres). With even the largest machine returning a claimed 62mpg, the range was considerable. A smaller 4-gallon (18-litre) tank was offered as an option, but did not have the elegant lines of the standard fitting and there seemed no good reason to choose one. The toolkit no longer lived in the

A smaller fuel tank was also offered on the R75/5 and its brothers.

tank but in a removable tray under the seat.

Almost unnoticed was the slimming exercise that accompanied the new range. In spite of the electric starter and the extra fittings, the new machines were all much lighter, with the R50 at 407lb (185kg) nearly 30lb (13kg) lighter than its predecessor. The R60 and the R75, both 418lb (190kg), showed a similar reduction.

The top speeds of the various models were actually lower than the bikes they replaced. The R50 was 3mph (5kph) slower than the old R50S at 97mph (157kph), the R60 was good for 103mph (167kph), 5mph (8kph) down on the R69S, whilst even the top of the range R75 claimed no higher a top speed, at 109mph (175kph), than the R69S. Performance was never fundamental to BMW and they could certainly have squeezed a little extra out of all the models had they so wished. The price for this, however, would have been less flexibility and little practical advantage.

The new machines had no trouble in maintaining their reputation as the most expensive motorcycles on the market for there was a massive price increase. In addition to electric starters and flashing indicators, a selection of colours was now available. Naturally, a black model held pride of place but white and silver, soon to be followed by a variety of colours, emphasised that these were not just *new* machines, but also *different* machines made under a philosophy almost alien to BMW.

Maybe some BMW riders recoiled in horror. Indeed, the traditional pre-/5 series models quickly became known as the 'pre-plastic' models as BMW had decided to use plastic mudguards. It was easy enough to ignore the extra weight and the problems of rotting (admittedly after many years' use) that characterised the traditional metal mudguards. Many of those who stuck to the older models (including the author) disguised their inability to afford such luxu-

ries by branding electric starters as 'sissy'! A revolution had indeed taken place. It was to be another fourteen years before the next one came along.

THE MAUDES TROPHY

During the next decade the /5 series was to revert to the traditional BMW pattern of few and subtle changes, each series of modifications being accompanied by a new number. In 1973 the /6 series was introduced but, just before that, the /5 benefited by increasing the wheelbase by 2in, and the arrival of a long-wheelbased /5 became a benchmark. The change was given considerable publicity when the first of the new models arrived in Great Britain as a challenger for the coveted Maudes Trophy, last won by Honda by 1963.

The Maudes Trophy was awarded for outstanding motorcycling achievement. The arbiters were the A-CU who, in this case, had been to Berlin to select three machines at random from the production line. The parts of the machines had then been marked with paint to prevent unauthorised changes. Two would be used for the attempt and the third would act as a reserve.

At this time the machines were imported by BMW (Concessionaires) GB, who decided that an attempt would be made to circulate the Isle of Man TT course for seven days and nights, stopping only for fuel and servicing. A team of British journalists (including the author), supplemented by road racers and friends, travelled to the Isle of Man in May 1973, and the white machines began their epic trip. They were flagged off the line by the legendary Geoff Duke, a resident of the Isle of Man. It would have been pleasant to report that the machines circulated without a hitch for the entire seven days, but nature, human and otherwise, intervened.

As thousands of pilgrims to this Mecca of motorcycling well know, the weather of this

New instrumentation but still drum brakes on the 1973 R60/6.

small island in the Irish Sea can be uncertain at the best of times. The week chosen for the TT saw some of the worst weather possible. It rained most of the time, and night laps across the famous Mountain Course invariably took place under heavy clouds, with rabbits and sheep wandering freely to add to the excitement.

There was no set speed planned but it was hoped to average around 50mph (80kph) for the week. Very soon the team managers were more concerned to keep the machines intact then to break the TT lap-record. This injunc-

tion did not deter TT winner Tony Jeffery – now a BMW dealer in Yorkshire – from circulating the touring R75/5s at lap-speeds of over 70mph (113kph) in the pouring rain and at night. Lesser mortals settled for lap times between thirty and forty minutes, which was still fast for the 37¾ mile circuit, especially as it had been stressed that all speed limits and traffic lights (there was only one set, just past the Grandstand) must be obeyed, an injunction that received varying degrees of acceptance. It was inevitable that, sooner or later, someone would make a mistake. Two

Geoff Duke and a bike he didn't ride – a cross-country version of the R60/2.

accidents occurred in quick succession.

During the fourth night, one of the team hit a rock at Brandish Corner, sending the machine cartwheeling down the road. Fortunately, the rider escaped without any serious injury. Frantic work by the BMW mechanics, led by Alberto Criscolo, had the badly-damaged bike back on the road in just four hours. It looked a little battered but still went well – though not for long. Road racer Mick Hemmings had flown in to relieve *Motor Cycle News* man Mike Nicks, and within a mile of taking over in torrential rain the BMW collided with the corporation dust-cart on Bray Hill. Hemmings was not seriously hurt but the front of the bike took on a shape never envisaged by the designers. Once again the mechanics performed miracles and only another four hours were lost.

Mechanically the bikes functioned perfectly, although the machine involved in the accidents had to have its clutch replaced: a consequence of the throttle sticking open after the collision. After seven days of almost non-stop riding the two machines had jointly covered 16,658 miles at an average speed, including all stops, of just under 50mph (80kph) Fuel consumption worked out at between 45 and 50mpg. Even after the demanding ride, neither machine produced any oil stains on the engine. One strange consequence of seven days and nights of non-stop use was that both seats were worn out, partly due to two members of the team being economy-sized policemen.

The team members suffered a long wait before being told that the A-CU did indeed consider the attempt worthy of the Maudes Trophy. (This trophy has only been won once more since then.) Perhaps the time is ripe for BMW to attempt to win it back.

THE FIRST EVER 900

Rumours about a 900cc BMW had been circulating since 1963. Indeed, the existence of both 750cc and 900cc prototypes had first been mentioned in the *BMW Club Journal* at that time. During the late 1960s 'interesting' models had begun to appear at BMW club gatherings in the Isle of Man and knowledgeable BMW watchers were of the view that some of the machines present were definitely larger than the then biggest machines made, which were 600cc.

It is characteristic of the company that they should hold something back when presenting the new /5 series to the world in 1969, and by 1973 the time was right for stimulating interest in the marque. Production at the Spandau works was now over 25,000 machines a year and there were plans to increase the capacity of the factory. Sales needed to be kept high and a series of changes, some minor, some less so, were announced.

The R60/6 and the R75/6 were launched as similar models to those made previously. The R50/5 was dropped. The R60 remained unchanged on the whole except that a five-speed gearbox was now specified, a change that would apply to all boxers right up to the present day. Perhaps 'unchanged' is an understatement, for the generator now produced 280 watts and – on the 600 only – the large fuel tank was replaced by the previously optional smaller one. Fuel-tank size was often a little confusing with BMWs at this time for, although the smaller tank was specified for the R60/6, most surviving models seem to have the larger tank. Also some R75s were supplied with the smaller tank. Thankfully the dreadful chrome side-panels that had been a less attractive part of

the /5s now gave way to matching ones that looked far better. The performance was unchanged. Characteristically the weight of the bike had crept up again and it now turned the scales at 440lb (200kg), 22lb (10kg) more than the /5.

Much the same modifications applied to the new R75/6, but with one important addition: a single-disc front brake was now specified, the first to be used on a production BMW. The weight of the 750 was also up by the same amount as that of the smaller bike, and performance was virtually unchanged.

It was the 900s that were the attention grabbers, though. The R90S was an immediate crowd-pleaser and has now been recognised as one of the classic BMWs. Finished in a stunning smoked-grey (a less stunning smoked-orange left traditionalists bewildered) it came with twin-disc brakes, a

Another 'classic' was the R90S, offered in either smoke grey or orange. The grey was truly handsome but had temperamental Dellorto carburettors.

Simplicity of design was still the theme even with high-performance BMW engines.

*Twin-disc brakes were offered for the
first time on the R90S.*

*Riding the R90S in Derbyshire in
1974.*

small cockpit fairing and the most powerful engine yet produced by the company. A rare departure from the use of Bing carburettors came with the fitting of Italian Dellortos. They looked good and worked very well when on song, but owners frequently had cause to curse their tendency to go out of balance – particularly unpleasant on a flat twin. The engine had a maximum power output of 67PS at 7,000rpm, enough to propel the new 900 at in excess of 125mph (200kph). No production BMW had ever offered such high performance. Nearly 24,000 examples were made during the three-year production run. Inevitably the R90S was also the heaviest bike now made, turning the scales at 451lb (205kg) but it did have the fairing and extra disc to add to its weight.

Launched at the same time was the 'cooking' version, the R90/6. It lacked

the eye-catching appeal of the S but was, for many touring riders, a better buy. Just one disc was considered enough for the 117mph (188kph) top speed and there was no fairing, just comfortable touring handlebars. Apart from the disc brake and constant depression carburettors, the R90 was virtually identical to the R60 and R75. Even the weight was the same and all models used a common crankcase and bottom end. Power output of the 'soft' 900 was 60PS at 6,500rpm and the 9:1 compression ratio was identical to that of the R75.

Not having a cockpit fairing on the R90/6 was offset by the fact that, for the first time for many years, BMW included in their catalogue a touring handlebar screen. It offered far more protection than the cockpit fairing, which was little more than a cosmetic exercise. The new screen was easy to fit (and even

Introduced as part of the /6 range, the 898cc R90/6 had a single-disc front brake and a choice of tank size.

easier to demolish if the rider fell off!) and is still a popular extra for many owners.

The R90/6 was much cheaper than its more glamorous partner, and almost exactly the same number were sold. Over 26,000 R75s were also sold but it was the R60 that set the sales charts alight, over 55,000 being purchased. Clearly, not all BMW owners were impressed by high performance and matching price tag.

IMPROVING THE BREED

Every motorcycle manufacturer who enters racing does so to improve his product, and nowhere are lessons learned more quickly or more painfully than on the race track.

BMW involvement in road racing in the 1960s had been low key and it was only as the new generation machines became established that the company dipped its toes, ever so cautiously, into racing waters.

Production racing had been introduced into the Isle of Man TT in the late 1960s and a development rider with Metzeler tyres, Helmut Dahne, earned the cheers of the crowd in 1974 when he not only rode his R75 into third place in the Production TT, but also rode it all the way from Munich and home again. To many it was exactly what they wanted to know – that this machine was capable of being ridden both on the road and on the track.

In 1976 Dahne went one better when he was joined by Hans-Otto Butenuth in the

Helmut Dahne, one of the most popular BMW racers, takes his R90S to victory in the 1976 Isle of Man Production TT.

1,000cc Production race. Once again BMW amazed the pundits by coming home in first place. Dahne, who was a part-time racer, continued to return to the Isle of Man throughout the 1970s and more than held his own even whilst riding uncompetitive machinery. Although he had a degree of support from BMW, he was his own man and rode the bikes that suited him, even to the detriment of race results. He even used his standard road suspension. Such an approach endeared him even more to BMW fans and he

was always a popular visitor to the island. He is still involved in motorcycling and every year gives the benefit of his experience to riders who attend the BMW Better Riding School at the Nürburgring in the Eifel Mountains.

Whilst Dahne was flying the flag in the Isle of Man, an Englishman based in the United States was one member of a team riding a special 750 prepared by the American importers Butler & Smith. His name was Reg Pridmore and the very fast 750s

Steve McLaughlin and Reg Pridmore score a spectacular victory in the 1976 superbikes race at Daytona Beach, USA.

achieved more success than even they would have believed possible, winning the American Motorcyclist Association Superbike Championship in 1974.

Back home, London dealers Gus Kuhn began to shift their allegiance from Norton to BMW and prepared a very successful production racer, emulating the MLG feat of the previous decade when they won the production class in the 1973 Barcelona 24-hour race. They raced BMWs with moderate success throughout the early part of the 1970s, but it was becoming clear that modern superbikes were now much faster than anything being produced by BMW. The end of BMW's racing involvement was inevitable.

9   1,000cc and a Full Fairing

Three years after reaching what seemed to be the optimum size for a twin-cylinder boxer engine, BMW took the concept a stage further and added another forty-one cubic centimetres to each cylinder to produce the biggest engine yet: the R100. This was achieved by increasing the bore from 90 to 94mm giving a capacity of 980cc. The stroke remained constant throughout the range at 70.6mm. Still designated the /7 series the greatest change came to the top of the range model, the R100RS, which was given a full fairing. It was immediately acclaimed as the best ever fairing on a motorcycle (whilst duly acknowledging the efforts of the Ariel Leader and the Vincent Black Prince), being incredibly stable at high speed and yet offering the rider a high degree of protection. Another virtue was that it *looked* the part. It was a true sporting fairing that worked, and so successful was the wind tunnel tested design that it was used on the BMW boxers with virtually no change until the arrival of the new generation boxes in 1993.

BMW have always produced what could be described as 'compromise' sports machines, offering high performance but still managing to keep bikes looking much the same as all the others. There was no such compromise with the new RS, and how could there be with such an elegant fairing? Initially, the model was shown with what amounted to a 1½ seat – the designers thinking it would appeal more to the solo rider. Maybe pillion passengers have more influence than was thought, for the optional dual-seat soon became the norm. It is now rare to see an RS with the shorter seat.

Journalists flew out from a parched England at the end of the summer of 1976 to a wet and green Bavaria. It was a welcome relief after the heat of the superb summer, but more important was the opportunity to discover the performance of the RS on German *autobahns*, and to find out if the fairing really kept the wet off.

It was an outstanding success. The RS's top speed was still claimed as being 125mph (200kph) but it was now a speed that could be held for as long as there was fuel in the tank (and no speed limits!). Some testers found the dropped handlebars a little too severe, but it was one of the few criticisms of a model that survived fourteen years – the longest-lived model ever from BMW (even if it was dropped for a few years).

Power output was now 70PS at 7,250rpm. The barriers were being pushed back even further, for both figures were the highest yet. Cast wheels were featured for the first time on a BMW, initially just on the RS. Production problems meant that these took longer coming than expected, and the first versions were built with spoked wheels.

Three 1,000cc models were introduced in 1976. In addition to the RS was the R100S, initially of 65PS but a year later bearing an engine identical to that of the RS. This was, in effect, an uprated R90S and included a cockpit fairing and the plastic rear-end

The first ever fairing from BMW (1976). The R100RS is still a favourite today.

behind the seat, which provided a small storage compartment. There was actually a slight drop in power output, for the complicated Dellortos, good as they were, were discarded for constant depression Bing V94s, identical to those used on the RS. Undoubtedly the most attractive feature of the new R100S was its colour, a deep smoked-red that gave the bike a touch of real class. (Other colours featured in the catalogue.)

Three 'cooking' models completed the range: the R60, R75 and R100. The R60 and R75 engines were little changed from the original /5's and the same power output was quoted. A bigger dualseat was used, eliminating the plastic tail of the sports models. One change that took a little getting used to was the introduction of new rocker covers. Gone was the stylish two-fin rounded cover and in its place came a deeper cover, which was finished in cast alloy, lacquered on the touring machines and gloss black on the two sports ones.

Although the specification of some of the models appeared to be identical to the original /5's there were a number of subtle

The cockpit of the BMW R100RS, based on aerodynamic principles, offers the rider maximum protection, reduces front wheel lift and minimises the yawing movement.

changes. The switchgear was on its third option, but left testers complaining that the one it replaced was better. The instruments were improved. The first R75 had a tachometer inset into the speedometer; a neat arrangement but long-sighted riders could hardly see the needle. Now large twin instruments were standard. Only the two S models had twin-discs, although a second disc was offered as an option on the rest, as was a kickstarter. There was continual refinement to the engines and the 750s were now smoother than the original.

BMW were still doing what they had always done, introducing changes yet doing so without noticeably changing the product – except, perhaps, when they tackled things such as rocker covers: a decision not universally acclaimed. As usually happens, a new

breed of BMW riders was coming along who couldn't see what all the fuss was about.

Until 1976, any motorcyclist who wanted to use his machine for touring was forced to buy proprietary brand panniers and bolt them on as best he could (again, the Ariel Leader must be mentioned as an honourable exception). There were some excellent panniers around but the fittings were often less than perfect and there could be problems with the machine's handling if they were not properly fitted.

Another first was scored by BMW when, from 1976 onwards, they offered panniers as an optional extra. Designed by Krauser especially for the bike, they were stylish and quickly detachable, and whilst some did leak occasionally, they were generally acclaimed by those who used them.

111

The Steib was finally bolted to a R100/7 and finished in matching smoke red. In spite of it being over thirty years old it is still one of the best-looking sidecars around.

Somewhere under this luggage is the R100/7-Steib outfit, here seen in Portugal.

Few riders using Krauser panniers on their machines realise that Mike Krauser, who designed them, was a successful racer. In 1956 he raced a banking sidecar similar to the design used before the war by a famous British racer, Freddie Dixon.

Strangely, few manufacturers regard the provision of luggage carrying facilities on a motorcycle as of any great importance. It is not an attitude shared by BMW, for they pick up more than their fair share of customers who appreciate such facilities.

EXIT THE 750

Eight years after the R75 heralded the BMW revolution it fell victim to it when it was replaced by the R80/7. Two versions were on offer: the 'normal' one producing 50PS at 7,250rpm, and what the Germans called the *Superkraftstoff* which produced 55PS at 7,000rpm. In Great Britain, it was the higher performance machine that was sold. German insurance laws made it desirable to keep

the power below 50PS, which was why the version was listed. Seen as a compromise between the powerful 1,000 and the sweeter 750, the R80 was an immediate success and has been making friends ever since. Police forces, particularly, liked the unflappable nature of the new 785cc bike and many thousands have been sold both to them and to the public. One might have wondered why BMW felt the need to increase the capacity of the R75, for no power or performance gain but for a less good fuel consumption. The reason given at the time was that it was an attempt by BMW to reduce noise levels, the larger capacity being quieter.

One year later, the company went to the other end of the spectrum by introducing the smallest boxer they had ever made. It was the 473cc R45. It was only 21cc smaller

Enjoying the R80/7.

Expect to meet more than your share of potholes in Ireland. Little has changed since this photograph was taken in 1980.

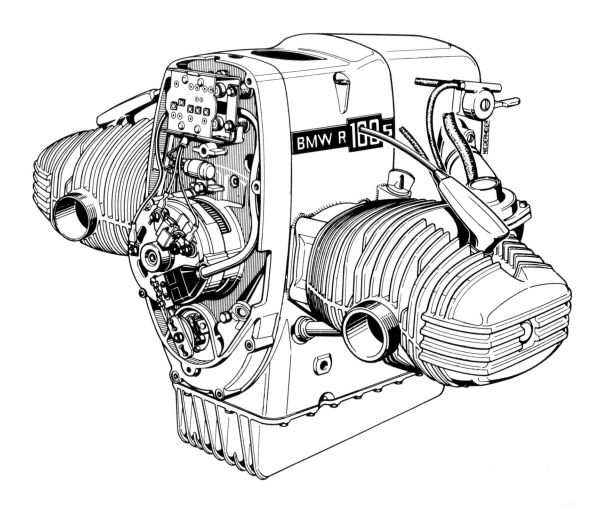

The BMW series horizontally opposed engine.

than the short-lived R50/5, and once again it was German insurance categories that encouraged this development, for a special low-power R45, producing 27PS at 6,500rpm, was made especially for the German market. It was sadly lacking in performance, and the export version with 35PS was hardly better – which just goes to show how demanding riders had become, for the export model produced the same power as the acceptably fast R50S introduced eighteen years previously. Weighing in at 450lb (205kg) it was barely heavier than the R50S and top speed

was identical at 100mph (160kph). With faster, more powerful models available, the R45 was not a success.

It was a different story with the R65, which was launched at the same time. Weighing exactly the same, the 650cc R65 (at last the designation exactly equated to the capacity) had a top speed of 108mph (175kph) and a forgiving nature. Both machines were seen as lightweight BMWs but both actually weighed little less than the R80/7.

To complement the smaller bikes came a full-blown tourer, the R100RT, and this time

Two years after the sporting R100RS came the R100RT, a touring bike that did not appeal to those who wanted style; it did appeal to the long-distance tourist.

the fairing was in the touring style. It cocooned the rider inside its ample proportions, and the riding position was a comfortable 'sit-up-and-beg'. Alongside this came the R100T, a slightly less powerful version without a fairing. Both machines were a development of the R100/7, although the RT used the more powerful R100RS engine.

There was a mixed reception for the new RT. Some road testers dismissed it as being too bulky, and its reluctance to respond to the knee-scraping demands of the boy racers was considered a fault. Serious touring riders took a different view, appreciating its long-distance capabilities. Many riders, especially older ones who had long appreciated the virtues of a BMW, were won over by the fairing's ability to keep the worst of the weather off. The adjustable windscreen height even took account of human beings' different sizes. The author has long been an unashamed fan of the RT and is happy to have one in his garage.

Considering the extra weight – it turned the scales at 462lb (209kg) – and frontal area, the RT was surprisingly fast, having a top speed of 118mph (190kph). Some interesting extras had begun to appear including a Nivomat self-adjusting rear-suspension. It did not have the delicacy of control of the standard units, but by some clever hydraulics it was able to adjust itself to suit the weight of the rider, passenger and luggage. It is an underrated option that is still available. More obviously luxurious were heated handlebar-grips – a much appreciated addition for winter riders – and hazard warning lights. Even a pump was still supplied though its days were numbered.

It has to be said that some strange colours crept into the BMW catalogue over the years. Few chose what was called 'curry' when it was offered on the /6 series. For the RT, a deep bottle-green was listed that would never, ever sell in a shipping town; its inhabitants were superstitious about such things. Initially the RT was offered in a two-tone brown and cream that could be considered rather boring. On the other hand, the smoked-red was delightful.

Just one more piece in the roadster boxer jigsaw remained to be fitted before the picture was complete and this was the introduction, in 1982, of the R80RT. It was almost an economy version of the R100 and lacked its clock and voltmeter. As if to emphasise the fact that it was not quite as good as the 1,000, the rocker covers were left unpainted, as indeed were the ones on all but the R100RT and R100RS. One would have thought it better economics to have finished all the rocker covers in black. BMW, however, are ever conscious of image and recognise the need to indicate which models have cost most money.

GELÄNDESTRASSE

Cross-country riding is an unlikely area for a

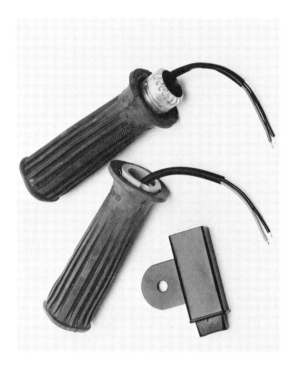

Much appreciated by winter-riding BMW people were heated handlebar grips.

big, heavy machine such as the BMW to excel in but, almost from the start of production, the company pursued the twin paths of road and off-road competition for their sporting aspirations. It was even more impressive that they often used the same riders in both sports. Ernst Henne, George Meier and Walter Zeller were amongst the many top road racers who were equally successful in cross-country events, and all won gold medals in ISDT. Such an award is hard enough to win on a lightweight machine that can be dragged or lifted clear of deep mud; on a BMW the only way out is to ride it and the sight of these big machines, which continued to compete in the ISDT long after most manufacturers had gone over to lightweight bikes, was always guaranteed to set the pulses racing.

A big machine usually needs a big man

An 800cc version of the RT (1982).

(but there was a notable later exception) and they rarely came bigger than Sebastian Nachtmann, who first rode a BMW in the ISDT in 1955. By the 1960s he was a star, blazing a path through the deepest mud and rockiest hills as he took the big BMW to numerous golds, usually setting the fastest time in special tests. Ken Heanes, Britain's team captain in the 1965 ISDT held in the Isle of Man (and, later, manager of the successful Maudes Trophy attempt) was reported in the motorcycle press as doing 90mph (145kph) on his Triumph Trophy in the speed test when big Sebastian went past him 'like a dose of salts'.

BMW continued their ISDT involvement at a reduced level throughout the 1970s, and riders such as Helbert Scheer, Herbert Scheck and Kurt Distler rode them with distinction. By the middle of the decade

Two R80GSs in their natural environment in Somerset.

Scheck had been involved in the production of a real monster. It was designated the GS80, and with a capacity of 872cc it was very special indeed: it was incredibly fast yet also smooth, and it would pull from very low revs. It just showed what could be done when money was no object and when every component of the bike was given special treatment. By 1979 the GS80 was beginning to look right and even had monoshock suspension; Fritzel won the over-750cc award in the ISDT, held that year in Poland. The blueprint for the R80GS was there.

All this experience was useful but few thought it could be turned into commercial success. Yet, in 1980, journalists from all over the world went to Avignon in France for the unveiling of the R80GS. It would be misleading to say that the new machine came as a shock, for there had been no shortage of 'hints' about a new off-road bike.

In spite of this the appearance of a machine that was, to a sober company like BMW, outlandish yet so correct left those lucky enough to be the first to ride it bubbling with enthusiasm. Few were under any illusions that it was a *serious* off-road bike, for even at a light 368lb (167kg) it was thought to be somewhat of a handful on the rough. And yet the test circuit included some miles of reasonable off-road going and the bikes performed admirably.

Two photographs of the second generation Geländestrasse, *the R80GS has a softer engine than that used on the 1,000.*

It was on the road that the GS earned its spurs, though, for it had all the attributes of a good off-road bike: wide handlebars and 'sit-up-and-beg' riding position, a smooth and flexible engine, long suspension travel and a tight steering-lock. The machine, almost unaccountably, blended into something really special for road use.

BMW had not used the centre-mounted monoshock suspension seen on the prototypes but a single swinging-arm unit, mounted on the right-hand side, with the rear wheel on a stub axle. To eyes unaccustomed to such a sight it was strange. Instinct suggested that it would make a lop-sided bike. It did not, of course, and the idea was later adopted for use on all the boxers.

Power for the R80GS (GS meaning *Geländestrasse*, which loosely translates as cross-country and road) came from the R80. A kickstarter only was supplied, with a 9-amp battery considered ample enough to trigger the new breakerless electronic ignition. An electric starter was an optional extra, an arrangement which also meant fitting a 16-amp battery. Understandably, the weight saved by dispensing with the electric starter and using a small battery would be considered an advantage for serious cross-country use. Maybe Sebastian Nachtmann had been the role-model for kickstarting the machine in standard trim, for a demonstration at the Avignon launch suggested that the easy way for normal human beings to operate the short (and awkward) kickstarter was to stand on the left cylinder. Few owners regarded the saving in weight as important, and the electric starter soon became standard.

Especially appreciated was a new lightweight clutch. The flywheel was forty per cent lighter and, coupled with the lighter clutch mechanism, it went a long way towards eliminating the BMW clunk – and gave the bike a revviness that was quite unlike any other produced by the company.

Spoked wheels were used, the cast wheels fitted to most other models being considered unsuitable for off-road use, which could get expensive if a rim was dented. To cater for off-road requirements the front wheel was 21in with an 18in rear wheel, both equipped with dual-purpose tyres more suitable for road use than track. Serious users of the GS, and there were quite a few owners entering long-distance trials, soon fitted trials tyres.

A front single-disc brake was thought to be more cosmetic than functional, for convention suggested that the idea was not practical for off-road use. With the benefit of hindsight, drum brakes were also of limited use and the disc has shown itself to be better than expected, being at least as good as drum brakes off-road and much better when used on tarmac, especially if the machine was used two-up with luggage. The image created of the bike was that of a machine you could tour on and many owners found it ideal for the task.

A new tank was created that held 4.25 gallons (19.5 litres); the exhaust system was of the siamesed type with a high level silencer that exited on the left and a plastic cover more or less protected the rider's legs from the heat. The exhaust system sounded beautiful but was prone to rotting, and growing numbers of riders are replacing it with a stainless steel type, available as a non-standard part, at much the same price.

The original colour was white with, unaccountably, an orange seat. It was hard to escape the feeling that this was mere whimsy by the designers. Strangely, the models that are still around seem to have kept the seat colour. It was not long, however, before a dark blue version with a black seat was added, a colour scheme that was as conservative as the other one was gaudy. A seat height of 34in (864mm) was enough to encourage riders to keep going, for extra long legs were needed to reach the ground, especially in adverse conditions.

Even on a bike that was ostensibly for off-road use, BMW paid careful attention to details. A clock and tachometer were options, as was a pannier set – the left side pannier recessed because of the high level silencer. Long-distance tourers soon learned to keep their pyjamas in that one.

BMW were undoubtedly ahead of the pack with their new R80GS. It was the largest capacity off-road bike ever produced in quantity. During the 1980s every big manufacturer would produce similar machines, mostly big singles or vee-twins that fell short of the BMW's 800cc. It was understood that only the foolhardy or intrepid would take seriously the off-road capabilities of these machines: most owners were content to *look* as though they had spent every weekend riding the bike in rugged terrain.

Many riders, the author included, consider that the R80GS was the best motorcycle produced by BMW in the 1980s. It was a delight to ride: the exhaust system, light clutch and new galnikal-coated aluminium cylinders contributed to a smoothness that made conventional boxers seem quite rough. It was not a totally practical machine, for the wide bars made high speed riding tiring. Any speed over 80mph (129mph) was not much fun. Long distances were likely to be a pain in the backside, both literally and metaphorically, especially for the passenger.

Neither problem mattered when using the R80GS in town – its tight steering-lock and flexible engine made it an ideal commuter – or in the country, whether the track was surfaced or not. These qualities no doubt contribute to the bike's endearing character.

Desert racing is another unlikely arena for the BMW, yet that is what the Paris–Dakar Rally entails. BMW entered a much-modified version of the R80GS in the 1981 event and, in the hands of Hubert Auriol, the R80GS won. Their machines came in fourth and seventh place. The victory was repeated in 1983, this time on a 1,000cc version. Success

Frenchman Hubert Auriol beat the world's best in 1983 to win the toughest bike event of all, the Paris–Dakar Rally, on this very special 1,000cc G/S.

did no harm to the sales of the GS, though in reality there was little similarity between the production R80GS and the one used by BMW in the Paris–Dakar race. In some countries, this model was the company's top-seller.

Auriol's win was repeated more than once. On the last occasion the diminutive Gaston Rahier, a below average-height rider, exploded the myth that only giants could ride a BMW successfully cross-country. Rahier proved that, above all, it was ability and bravery which counted.

FURTHER IMPROVEMENTS

Such had been the pace of development during the five years leading up to 1982 that, had BMW sat back and called it a day, it would not have caused any surprise. Everyone knew that a new water-cooled four was imminent so was there any point in continuing progress on the boxers?

In 1981, just a year after the launch of the R80GS, a new thousand, the R100CS, was unveiled. It was really an update of the R100S, the CS meaning Classic Sport. After the excitement of the new GS, the changes were quite mild. The aluminium cylinder

barrels introduced on the off-road bike were now added to all the boxers, including the CS, replacing the cast-iron ones. Also added was the lightweight clutch and – much appreciated by traditionalists – spoke wheels were recalled on the GS, CS and police specification R80s.

Just two years away from the new K-series, more was still to come. When the R80GS was launched there was a concerted cry for a road version. This came in July as the R80ST and, as is so often the case when a machine is produced by popular demand, it was not a success and attracted lukewarm reviews.

It was, in fact, a bit of a hybrid. The GS

The R100CS, successor to the R100S, was a stylish sports tourer using the same engine as the R100RS.

Another view of the R100CS.

frame with its single leg suspension was used, as were the exhaust system and motor. A smaller front wheel took over from the 21in off-road one, utilising GS hub and CS rim. The R45/65 series contributed the close-fitting front mudguard. The instrument panel, halogen headlight and handlebars came from the American version of the R65. The result was a light 403lb (183kg), reasonably fast motorcycle with a top speed of 108mph (174kph) that did most things well but had no real attention-grabbing feature, although in 1982 one magazine voted it 'the most practical motorcycle of the year'. It remained in the catalogues for a few years, then was just quietly dropped – which was a

pity as it was a good middle-range bike, unlucky to be overshadowed by the macho GS.

Much more successful was the R80RT, a downmarket version of the R100RT that cut out some of the frills such as the clock and voltmeter. Perhaps because it was based on such a desirable touring concept, it survived until not too long ago. It used the same engine as that of the GS, featuring the now universal breakerless ignition, lightweight flywheel, increased clutch leverage (making for a very light clutch), and a torsion damper in the cardan shaft – an innovation introduced to try and overcome the criticism about the clunky gearbox. It worked after a

A very underrated machine – the R80ST.

The BMW R80ST.

The 800/1000 series boxer engine.

A true copy! The Japanese Marusho Magnum was strong on looks but short on orginality – just about a straight pinch.

fashion, but it was not until the lightweight flywheel was added that the criticisms of the gearbox stopped.

A hydraulic steering damper remained as standard and, to comply with the law in some European countries, a first-aid kit was fitted into a recess in the front of the seat, although many riders regretted the loss of padding. BMW had long been in the forefront when it came to horns and the two-tone ones used on the models in the 1980s were the best yet. Not surprisingly, the fairing increased the weight to 472lb (214kg), which in turn took its toll on the top speed, now only a shade over 100mph (160kph). Those who wanted something faster could still buy the 1,000cc version.

When the 1983 range was announced by BMW there were eight versions of the boxer sold in Great Britain. The ill-fated ST had disappeared but the R65LS, introduced in 1981, was still included. It was a half-

Not everyone went for the 'style' of the R65LS!

hearted attempt to transform a mainly staid, conservative machine into a more snazzy one. A small spoiler fairing, low handlebars and matt black chrome exhausts made for either a stylish bike or – depending upon one's perspective – one that was quite out of character for a BMW.

There were to be no more notable changes to the boxer for some time, for almost daily stories about the new water-cooled BMWs were reported. Those who had grown up with, and had great love for, an engine that was nearly seventy years old feared the worst and wondered if it meant the end of the boxer.

10　The Flying Brick

Long before the motorcycle press descended on the south of France in September 1983 to sample the new water-cooled BMW, the bike had earned the nickname of the Flying Brick. Any motorcycle magazine prepared to have a reporter sit for hours near the company's test circuit could snatch a photo, and even before the new machine was announced the grapevine revealed that the bike was a four and that a three-cylinder version was not far away. The grapevine was right. The photographs earned it its nickname, for a brick is exactly what the engine looked like.

It is impossible to describe the feelings of a traditional boxer man confronted with a machine so different, so un-BMW-like and so . . . frantic, that the only way to identify it was by the badge on the tank.

The company frankly admitted that the new K-series, as it was to be called, was designed to meet the Japanese challenge head-on. They had looked at the possibility of further developing the boxer unit but had concluded that it was not possible to produce more than 70PS from this engine configuration without unacceptable compromises. Nor would it be possible for much longer for the air-cooled unit to conform to noise and – soon to be introduced – emission regulations if adequate performance was to be extracted (ten years later they found a way of surmounting the environmental problems with the boxer). The new K-series had cost DM300 million (£100 million) to develop, an investment that would never have been possible without the resources of the car division.

Logic suggested that, to keep at least a tenuous connection to the horizontally opposed tradition, if the bike must be a four-cylinder engine, then it should be a flat four. Maybe it would have been, had the Honda Gold Wing not used the same configuration: BMW would not be seen copying the Japanese.

When designer Josef Fritzwenger decided that it would be an in-line four, but installed longitudinally and horizontally (in other words the engine was running front-to-rear but lying on its side so that the cylinder head pointed to the left), the decision to ensure that it was like no other motorcycle was at once logical and unique. It had the advantage of the centre of gravity being kept low whilst the crankshaft ran in the same direction as the drive shaft – a tradition that, thankfully, was not discarded. If BMW were guided a little along the road, or more truthfully not guided, by what other manufacturers were doing, they certainly were not saying.

It would have been considered a disaster had the new engine not produced more horsepower than the 1,000cc boxers, but its almost square (67×70mm) engine returned 90PS, giving the unfaired K100 a top speed of 132mph (215kph). The sports faired K100RS was just 3mph (5kph) faster; the touring version, the K100RT (which was to follow in 1984) was listed as having the same speed as that of the basic K100. It made them the fastest BMW motorcycles ever sold, a situation that continued until the introduction of the K1 six years later.

There can be no doubt that the bike was a sensation. In some respects it was no more

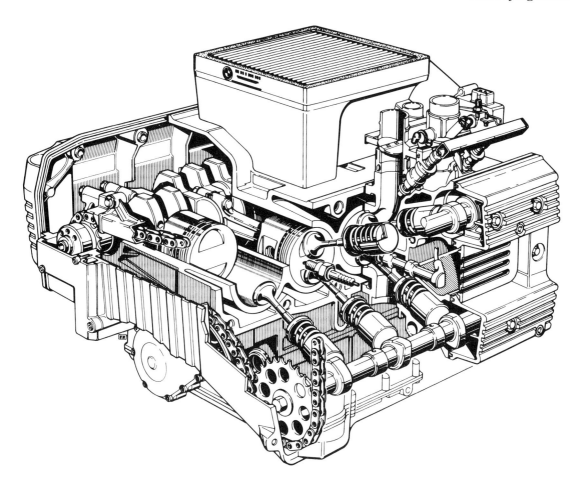

The longitudinally and horizontally installed four-cylinder in-line engine of the BMW K100.

technically advanced than the exotic Japanese machines on the market, and it was no more expensive either. What it did have was a superbly orchestrated launch where the world's press were given a wealth of technical detail and ample opportunity to quiz the people who had designed the machine. Naturally there was plenty of opportunity to ride it and discover that here was something truly different. It also had the appeal of tradition, and the company counted upon loyalty from its customers.

The value of that blue and white badge on the tank is inestimable. No matter how good the opposition, there is always that one extra that no one else has. The company expected that about half the customers for the new machines would come from the ranks of boxer owners. This has proved to be about right, although in later years many K owners have grown tired of all the complication and have returned to the boxer. Few other manufacturers can possibly hope for the same degree of loyalty.

Technically, the K was a masterpiece, with two onboard computers controlling ignition and fuel injection. Carburettors no longer figured in the plans of the designers of this

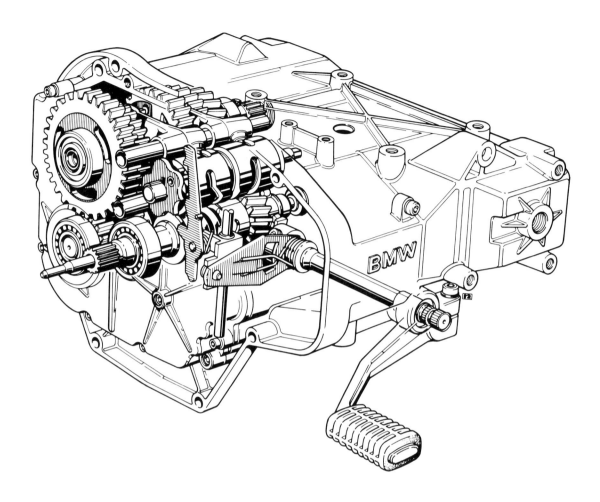

Three-shaft five-speed gearbox of the BMW K100 and K75.

new engine and distribution of the fuel mixture was now controlled by Bosch LE Jetronic, a system that has successfully been in use on BMW cars for some years. It incorporated a fuel cut-off on the overrun which, combined with more efficient fuel burning, gave far better fuel economy on the K-series machines than could be achieved on modern day boxers. Ignition was also by Bosch, using their VZ-51L digital system: the home mechanic would be hard put to tinker with the engine in the garage.

New heights were reached in the electrics with a generator that produced no less than

460 watts, a level of output that would prove invaluable five years later. Starting a four-cylinder engine demands much less of the starter and battery than a boxer and a 20 amp-hour battery was considered enough. Gone are the days of BMW engines groaning to turn over on cold mornings (at least for K owners).

A five-speed gearbox and shaft drive, now called the BMW Compact drive system, were nominally the same as that used on the boxers. In truth, not one part used on the boxer survived on the Ks.

The compact engine/gearbox unit forms

The state-of-the-art (at the time) K100RS with anti-lock brakes (ABS).

part of the frame, using what BMW call a tubular space frame with the engine as additional support. Even though the engine is water-cooled the unfaired K100 turned the scales at only 527lb (239kg) with a full fuel tank, making it the lightest one-litre four-cylinder motorcycle in the world. Even so it was 44lb (20kg) heavier than the unfaired boxer, the R100. There is always a price to be paid for progress. The K100RS, similar in concept to the boxer RS with lower handle-bars and a sporting fairing, weighed just 22lb (10kg) more.

When it comes to colour schemes BMW have always been strangely conservative (except for the occasional rush of blood to the head resulting in the orange R90S or the curry /5s!). Initially the K-series, both the naked K100 and the sporting K100RS, were offered in metallic silver. It was a neutral colour which neither offended nor pleased anyone. A year later the third 1,000cc K100, the RT, was introduced in dark grey or maroon. It followed the familiar BMW pattern of extending the range by offering a touring fairing. For the author it was the best of the water-cooled 1,000s offering protection and comfort alongside the smoothness of the new fours. It meant that, for the time being, BMW were content with their new Ks. As long as sales held up, and the factory was approaching full production, the new BMW was secure.

What of the boxers? It was confidently expected that the delightful flat twins, of which half a million had been made since 1923, would slowly be phased-out. Maybe that was the intention but initially the company announced that, in future, they would only make boxers for the 800cc class

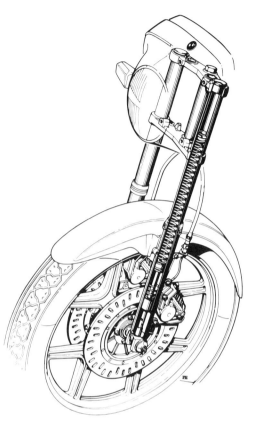

and below. It made sound commercial sense, for what was the point of competing with their own products? Boxer fans saw it as the beginning of the end but BMW said that, at least until a pattern emerged, the production line at Spandau would make sixty per cent water-cooled machines and forty per cent air-cooled ones.

A TRIPLE SUCCESS

The existence of the three-cylinder K-series BMW was common knowledge long before the first Ks were announced. Many stories were circulating as to why it was not launched at the same time as the 1,000. One version held that it was because the bike was faster than the K100 and would take sales from the new flagship. A more likely explanation is that BMW never put all their eggs in one basket. By delaying the launch of the K75 to 1985, the company were guaranteed another large bite of the publicity cherry. There was also the small matter of preparing

Front wheel of the BMW K100 with telescopic fork.

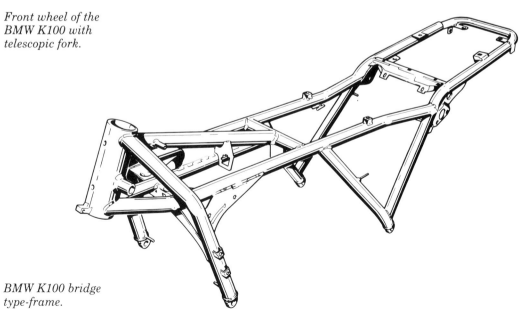

BMW K100 bridge type-frame.

and producing the machines, for it was suggested that BMW engineers were not completely satisfied with the 750: which explains why it was another two years before it appeared.

The formula for the new triple was simple. It was much the same as the K100, but with one less cylinder. Power output per litre was actually higher than that of the K100, for the new K75 produced 75PS compared to the 90PS of the 100. Subtracting one cylinder also removed 22lb (10kg) from the weight. As the three-cylinder engine does not have the natural balance of the fours, it also has two balance weights on the drive shaft. This revolves in the opposite direction to the crankshaft at exactly the same speed and, in the case of the K75, acts as an equalising shaft.

In many other respects the machines were identical, and over fifty per cent of the parts used in the K75 were common to the K100. But there were significant differences. The bore and stroke were identical to the 1,000 but the smaller bike had different valve timing, a modified combustion chamber, new pistons and a higher compression ratio. The electrics and main cycle parts were all the same and included the unusual self-cancelling indicators, with the rider using the left hand to operate the left signal and the right to operate the right. It took a little while to get used to, but most owners grew to like it.

Two models were announced: the K75C base model, and the K75S which had a sports fairing – this would not appear until the following June. Strangely, there was an unexpected difference between the K75C and the rest of the series (including the K75S) in that, where all the other models had a 17in rear wheel and disc brake, the C had an 18in rear wheel and a drum brake. All models used twin dual caliper discs for the front. The use of a different rear brake and wheel size seemed to conflict with the

company's 'building brick' system whereby parts would be interchangeable whenever possible. Top speed of the K75C was 124mph (200kph) and the K75S 130mph (210kph). To all intents and purposes, the performance difference between them was insignificant.

Within weeks of the launch of the K75C, the author and Terry Snelling, a reporter on the weekly paper *Motor Cycle News*, were flown to Narvik in the Arctic Circle and invited to ride two of the new machines to Gibraltar, a distance of 3,700 miles (5,953 kilometres), in ten days. The machines made light work of the journey, which started in the snow and finished in the scorching heat. However, the two riders, who were making a promotional video for BMW, found that the trip was not the sinecure that it sounded when first suggested. There was one day of rest during the journey and literally dozens

The frozen wastes of the Artic. The author and Terry Snelling of Motor Cycle News *rode these two K75Cs from Narvik to Gibraltar for a promotional video.*

K75C in Bavaria.

of stops for filming. An average of 411 miles (661 kilometres) a day were covered and the machines ran perfectly.

Interestingly, in spite of the high speeds necessary on such a ride, the fuel consumption for the 3,700 miles worked out at 57mpg. This excellent fuel economy was proving to be a real plus with the new K-series: only weeks before, the author had completed a 4,000-mile trip to Portugal on K100RT and this, too, averaged 57mpg for the journey – although not at quite such high speeds!

When the K75S was produced it proved to be a very different kettle of fish from the C. There was a small fairing, higher performance and much modified suspension which included a new front fork set-up that had damping in the left fork leg only. Both legs had springs but the right side contained just oil and acted as an air cushion. There was no

special reason for choosing the left side but BMW engineers said that it made oil flow and fine tuning of the front-suspension easier. A new matching single rear-suspension unit was also introduced, giving greatly improved handling but a much firmer ride.

Three-cylinder engines have a different feel to those with two or four and the K75 illustrates this perfectly. Although it is higher revving – producing its maximum power at 8,500rpm compared to the K100's 8,000rpm – it is a sweeter, somehow less frantic engine than the 1,000's. Certainly the author regards the ride from the Arctic Circle to Gibraltar as being one of the most enjoyable of his motorcycling career.

REFINEMENT

By the standards of a company which had always 'made haste slowly' the 1980s had been breathtaking, with BMW launching bikes in two vastly different directions. The water-cooled fours went for the luxury market and the dual-purpose GS eschewed such notions and offered riders the chance to take to the hills.

There was to be no slowing down, and in 1987 a new luxury tourer was included in the range, the K100LT. It was really just a logical development of the RT and acknowledged that riders at this end of the market wanted a few little extras in life. The machine came with full luggage equipment including a top box and, initially, provision for a radio.

Its *raison d'être* was high speed and comfortable travelling, with the rider protected from the weather and untroubled by wind pressure. Critics say that a machine such as the LT is no more than a two-wheeled car. Indeed it is, but many riders regard it as having many of the advantages of a car but fewer of the disadvantages.

In 1987 the machine was put to the test by

High on an Austrian mountain, not far from Bischofshofen, with the K100LT.

the author when, with his son Simon on the pillion, he rode 1,000 miles in a day, leaving Vlissingen in Holland at 7 a.m. and arriving near Vienna just after midnight, having travelled by way of Hamburg, Regensburg and Passau, a distance of 1,026 miles (1,940 kilometres). An average speed of 76mph (122kph) was achieved for the ride (not including stops) and the average cruising speed, whenever possible on Germany's unrestricted *autobahns*, was 110–120mph (177–193kph).

It was not an easy journey but the LT showed its mettle by delivering relatively unstressed riders at the end of the journey. Some of the trip was in heavy rain and one

lurid high speed slide near Nuremburg left rider and passenger subdued for a while. In this case the average fuel consumption for the trip worked out at slightly over 39mpg. The return trip, made at a more leisurely pace, saw the consumption improve to 52mpg.

Not long after the K100LT winged its way to Vienna, BMW should have been introducing their long awaited anti-lock brakes. The notion of anti-lock brakes on bikes had been around for many years but had never progressed beyond the prototype stage. BMW became the first to announce that they would be introducing a machine so equipped. It was first shown at the Cologne show in

Discovering that ABS really does work at RAF Gattow, Berlin.

September 1986 but, because of endurance testing difficulties, full scale production was delayed for what finally turned out to be eighteen months.

So it was March 1988 when a party of pressmen descended on Berlin to sample the world's first production anti-lock brake. Many paths had been trod in reaching what the company considered to be the optimum arrangement.

Martin Probst was given the credit for seeing the ABS (Anti-Blockier System) through to production. He had joined BMW in 1974 to become head of motorcycle design in January 1988. Prior to that he had been responsible for motorcycle development.

Anti-lock brakes were developed in co-operation with FAG Kugelfischer and were not the first option tried. The British Transport and Road Research Laboratory had been looking at anti-lock brakes for many years and had evolved a mechanical system that was well received but not taken up by any motorcycle manufacturer.

BMW looked long and hard at the idea of mechanical anti-lock brakes but, after many years of tests, finally decided that the most efficient way was electronically, with a 100-tooth impulse generator on each wheel. In effect this monitors the reaction of the brake seven times per second, fractionally releasing and reapplying the brake as the point of breakaway is approached. It is an extremely sophisticated arrangement and there can be no doubt that the mechanical device will be cheaper to make and easier to construct. However, BMW, aware of this, decided that only the best was good enough and it was the Anti-Blockier System that greeted riders in Berlin.

All of the invited riders were extremely experienced, and possibly most considered that they could get optimum braking from conventional brakes. Tests on an aerodrome circuit soon showed that this was not the case. Using a non-ABS BMW (equipped with skids), the machine was ridden hard at a mixture of wet sand and cement. Invariably

136

there came a time when the wheels locked under heavy braking. No matter who was riding, the ABS bike never locked its wheels no matter how hard the rider braked. It was an impressive demonstration.

What it did illustrate was that few riders get anywhere near their maximum braking point. The author has spent some time riding an ABS-equipped BMW. At no time during that period did he actually *need* anti-lock brakes but, by process of investigation and practice, he discovered that he was not using anywhere near the full braking power of the machine.

Anti-lock brakes are not the answer to foolish actions and if they are used as a performance aid there comes a point when even the brakes cannot help. However, for the mature motorcyclist who has the sense to use the brakes as they are intended, the BMW ABS system is magnificent and must be considered the motorcycling safety-aid of the decade. One thing will inhibit its introduction on other machines, though. Its demands on the electrical supply are such that even the 280-watt generator of the boxers is inadequate. It needs all of the 480 watts produced by the larger generator of the Ks to operate satisfactorily.

Anti-lock brakes are here to stay, but it is a matter of debate as to how soon they will be available to a wider circle of motorcyclists than owners of BMW and, more recently, some 'top of the range' Japanese models.

A TRUE SURVIVOR

Fears that the day of the BMW boxer was over were partly allayed by the BMW announcement, at the launch of the K-series in 1983, that they intended to continue to make flat twins in the under-800cc class. There was a certain amount of unhappiness amongst BMW buffs that the bigger machines had apparently been discarded but

this was eased by the announcement, in 1984, of revised versions of the R80, R80RT and the R80GS. The first machines were given the single-sided suspension that had been such a success on the GS, and all three had a modified engine that introduced a degree of smoothness not seen since the days of the R60/2. Detail work on the valve gear, a lightweight clutch and the lower-powered engine originally introduced for the German market resulted in such a smooth engine that riders began to wonder why it had not happened before. The answer is simple enough. It took over sixty years of refinement and honing to produce a boxer that was as near to perfection as BMW had yet achieved.

It was but a first step, for a year later the same treatment was given to the R65 and this, because it was smaller, achieved even sweeter results. It was just two PS down on the R80 and now had just 48PS at its command. Its predecessor produced 50PS and the BMW line was that this drop in power was to enable to new R65 to run on unleaded fuel. It does not seem too unreasonable to assume that it did not make commercial sense, either, to offer the R65 and the R80 with the same power output.

On all the boxers the rear wheel drive was now running on bevel gears similar to those used on the Ks. Previously, needle bearings were used, but the new arrangement was more reliable and able to take a higher load. On the smaller machine a single-disc front brake was considered enough – not a logical arrangement as its top speed was, at 107mph (173kph), a mere 3mph (5kph) slower than the R80 and weighed, at 451lb (205kg), only 11lb (5kg) less.

The introduction of monoshock suspension meant that every BMW made now used a stub axle. Rear wheel removal, never a chore on a BMW, was even easier. Diehards were less enthusiastic about the disappearance of the tyre pump: all machines used tubeless

By 1984 the R80RT had monoshock suspension and one of the smoothest BMW engines yet made.

tyres and three little air bottles replaced the pump. Cautious owners still carried a spare tube.

The motorcycling public, or at least those who say they represent them, had never stopped clamouring for the return of the 1,000cc boxers. In 1986 BMW reintroduced, by popular demand they say, the R100RS. A year later the R100RT and a newcomer, the R100GS, followed. The power output of the thousands was, as had become the practice, 'pegged', this time at 60PS, a 10PS reduction on the older R100's. It made sense, for now

BMWs were made with 48, 50, 60, 75 and 90PS options.

Both the road bikes joined the rest of the boxers in having monoshock suspension. In almost all respects they were identical to the R80s. Losing a few horsepower compared to the old R100s had done the new machines no harm at all. The motor was, without a doubt, the most pleasant in this class that the company had yet produced. The loss in top end performance was of little concern to those who bought the machine.

Just in case the new-found faith in the

Not really ideal for serious cross-country riding but a superb dual-purpose tourer – the R100GS.

boxers was seen as a flash in the pan there came, in 1987, a complete re-vamp of the *Geländestrasse* models. Quaintly, the designation lost the stroke between G and S. Perhaps this was to show that the relationship between the new and old models was changed 'at a stroke'. BMW said, on the introduction of the new series, that you could count the unchanged components on the fingers of one hand. Fortunately, the new GS still had cylinders poking out of the side but the changes were indeed considerable.

A stronger frame was introduced, and new, longer travel telescopic front forks by Marzocchi, who had supplied the forks for the successful Paris–Dakar machines.

Desert racing had shown the need for greater strength in the materials used, which included a particularly hard-wearing friction surface between inner and outer fork-tubes. To stiffen things up even more a new fork bridge was introduced. Small things received the same attention to detail – the front axle was now hollow, to reduce unsprung weight. A larger Brembo front disc also had improved hydraulics to reduce the lever pressure needed to make the brakes work.

The increasing demands made by cross-country BMW riders, particularly as many were converting the machines to 1,000cc, began to show up limitations in the rear-drive system. They had always been there but the greater demands of track riding high-lighted them. A new system was devised to overcome this. It was called the Paralever and, whilst the idea is simple enough to understand, experts and enthusiasts alike are still arguing about how it actually works.

What BMW have done is to introduce a second universal coupling into the drive shaft. This enables the machine to gain further advantage from the suspension without the need for an extra long rear unit. In essence, the Paralever works on the principle of a parallelogram with a robust torque arm enabling the rear shaft to move through two angles, thus giving the rear-suspension far longer travel (about seventy per cent more) than is normally available. It reduces the effects of accelerating forces to a minimum whilst ensuring that there is no dive during braking. BMW have doubtless solved a problem which few people realised

they had in the first place, and the average GS owner might frighten himself long before the advantages of the Paralever system can be felt.

For all that, the GS was now better able to cope with a wider variety of terrain than before – which was just as well, for the new engine, with the better breathing of two 40mm Bing constant depression carburettors, can be a fearsome beast when used for serious cross-country riding. A top speed of 112mph (181kph) for the R100GS provided more than ample road performance, given the wide bars and lack of protection from the elements. Thankfully the softer R80GS is still made for those who want to enjoy undemanding trail riding, although a top speed of 104mph (168kph) was not far behind the 1,000's.

The machines shared many common features: bright, not to say garish, colour

Ks and Rs on the same production lines in Spandau, Berlin.

Assembling the Ks in Spandau, Berlin.

schemes for a start, with the black and yellow of the R100GS being particularly eye-catching. Large fuel tanks have become a feature of many large capacity cross-country bikes and, with the introduction of the Paris–Dakar option of the R80 in 1984, the company really went over the top with a tank holding 7 gallons (32 litres). Seven gallons of fuel adds a lot of weight up top, but riders did appreciate having to stop for fuel less often. Few benefited from being able to travel well over 300 miles without a stop. On the new generation GSs a 5.7-gallon (26-litre) fuel tank was standard, with over a gallon in a reserve tank.

All the work carried out on the new machines had a great effect on weight and with the 1,000 turning the scales at 412lb (187kg) dry (463lb (210kg) ready for the road) it was the lightest 1,000 ever made by BMW. Indeed, of the twins made since the war only the original R80G/S could claim to weigh less. The new R80GS weighed exactly the same and this helped in no small part in establishing the dual purpose machines as serious contenders for road bike use. For most riders, taking the machines into the wilds means little more than badly surfaced roads in remote parts. There will always be handful of enthusiasts who will find deep mud, rocky hills and log strewn forests. It is not those who have made the GS such a success, though. It is riders who enjoy the light weight, the superb riding position and sheer style of the machine.

The story of the boxer looked as though its

final chapter was being written in 1983. Not any more. BMW expected to phase the flat twins out slowly, as the K-series replaced the air-cooled bikes with machines that were easier to make to conform to noise and emission regulations. There has now been a change of emphasis. Whilst at one time it was thought that the twins would never be able to reach increasingly stringent noise and emission standards, a reduction in power and continued development of the engines have shown otherwise. The revised air-cooled engines were made to conform to the new requirements and the production lines in Spandau were running parallel with almost as many boxers being made as Ks. There is room for both bikes in the BMW catalogue and the company would think long and hard before deserting the concept of the flat twin, as we were to discover ten years later.

BMW INTO THE 1990S

What would Max Friz have said, had he stood in the crowd at the 1988 Cologne Show and gazed at the latest BMW, the K1? Putting aside the initial feeling that he would have turned in his grave, his more likely reaction would have been one of approval. Didn't he, not once but many times, run ahead of the pack, introducing ideas and designs that were ahead of their time?

If BMW had set out to alienate as many of their supporters in one go as possible they could not have made a better job of it than with the new K1. It is everything that BMWs are supposed not to be: flash, futuristic, unconventional, stylish, bawdy and most definitely over-the-top. It is also the logical development of the four-cylinder concept; where else is there to go other than into direct competition with the Japanese super-bikes? When the K-series was launched in 1983 there was speculation as to how it would be greeted by the owners of Japanese

Not at all like a BMW! The futuristic K1 in Italy.

exotica – seen by many as the natural customers for a machine as advanced in design as the K. It is not easy to answer the question. No doubt many customers have been converted from Japanese machines, especially since they are often no cheaper. Times have changed, though. The latest motorcycles from the opposition are bright, stylish, very fast and they most definitely stand out in a crowd. For all the K's attributes, it does not achieve that kind of prominence, possibly because BMW tend to choose colours seemingly designed to ensure that it will not.

The arrival of the K1 changed all that. Who could fail to step back in wonder at a machine that comes in bright, bright red with yellow wheels and graphics? Add to that a style that screams out to the world to be noticed, and

The K1.

you have a BMW unlike any other. Almost apologetically, a second offering in dark blue with yellow graphics and wheels shows that to make a bike like the K1 and then play down its attributes just doesn't work.

The basis of the new bike was still the four-cylinder water-cooled K engine, but it has four valves per cylinder and Digital Motor Electronics similar to that used on BMW cars. Normally such an arrangement would narrow the power band of an engine; but not so on the K1. A broad power curve and maximum torque at 6,750rmp makes for an incredibly flexible engine. Although the K1 is by far the fastest production BMW ever made, with a top speed approaching 150mph (241kph), it will pull equally well from 15mph (24kph) in top gear.

A voluntary German power limit of 100bhp

means that this is the top figure produced by the new machine. BMW engineers say that as this gives a top speed of 150mph (241kph) there is no advantage other than that of publicity in building a bike with more power. The clear implication is that, should BMW wish to increase the power output to, say, 125PS then it can do so.

A strengthened frame, stainless steel silencer and the Paralever rear-drive system (first introduced on the R100GS, showing that cross-fertilisation exists even between the Rs and the Ks) contribute to the technical excellence of the bike. Even the weird-looking front mudguard adds to the wind-cheating properties of the K1, a slipperiness that needs outstanding brakes to bring it to a halt. Twin-discs, drilled for lightness, with dual-piston operation and

Rome provided the setting for the launch of the image-breaking K1. It grabbed a lot of headlines but few customers, and is no longer made.

geometry normally found only on racing bikes means that the K1 had the best brakes ever fitted to a BMW. ABS was supplied on most K1s and became a standard fitting on all as the units became available. With a weight of 568lb (258kg) the machine is not a lightweight.

Futuristic is an easy word to slip in when trying to describe the K1, but it is just that. A new fairing has a coefficient drag of 0.4. This measure of the bike's ability to slip through the air is the best ever for a motorcycle and compares very favourably with Formula 1 racing cars. In practice it means that the rider is better protected than ever before with the added bonus of even better

performance. Although the top speed of the new machine is approaching that of the racing look-alikes it achieves this with only 8,000rpm, no more revolutions than are required by the K100RS.

At almost any speed the rider is cocooned in a secure shell, untroubled by the air outside hurtling by at any speed up to the maximum. A riding position not unlike that on the K100RS feels somehow more comfortable thanks to an excellent relationship between the handlebars (these are wider than the sports bars previously used on sporting BMWs), seat and footrests. So well covered is the engine by the shell that a blast of hot air ensures that the rider's left buttock

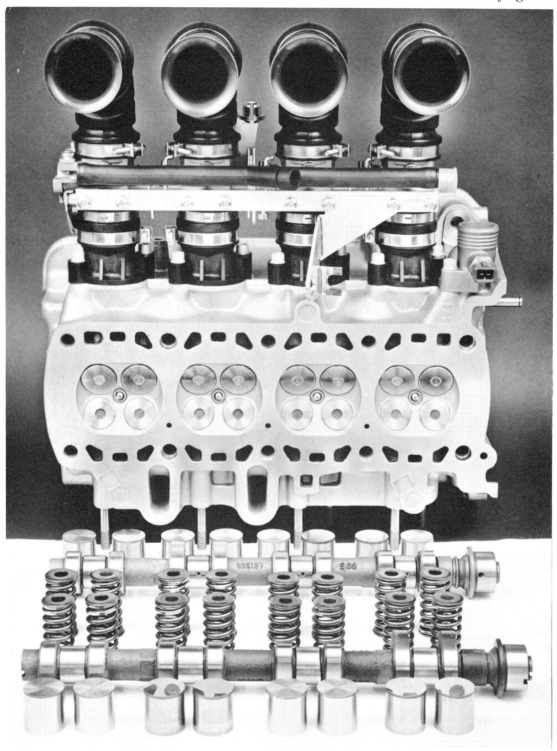

Sixteen valves are a feature of the K1.

is permanently on the warm side. Not quite an Achilles heel, but moving in that direction.

At this stage of development BMW made no pretence that the new K1 was for anything other than hedonistic use. There *was* a pillion seat but a miniscule provision for luggage – by way of two small panniers situated at the rear – means that the only place for anything other than a change of underwear was on the pillion seat. Special BMW bags were offered to encourage this.

Have no doubt, the new K1 was not the final page in the BMW story and it can only be a matter of time before the new four-valve engine found its way into the rest of the K-series. In many ways the new flagship was almost a challenge to convention. This is BMW's way of saying that it is easy to make a flashy bike, but that only a company with their skills, knowledge and experience can make one that is in one throw both visually outrageous and yet mechanically right.

Having proved their point, it was not too long before the K1 was dropped from the catalogue. It was a very interesting motorcycle but not a popular one, so it had to go. It came in like a lion but went out like a lamb.

11 The Changing Nineties

With the end of the 1980s came a new era for BMW, one that saw them looking at surprising new horizons. BMW owners had not only survived the shock of BMW making a liquid-cooled four-, and later three-cylinder engines, but had embraced it enthusiastically. These new bikes brought a whole new breed of riders into the fold, ones who had never ridden a 'traditional' boxer, and, perhaps, had no great desire to do so.

Not too far ahead BMW owners would be offered a totally 'new' boxer but for now it was the K-series liquid-cooled motorcycles that received all the attention. When the uncharacteristic K1 was introduced in 1989 it used a new, more powerful four-valve engine. Now it was being made available in a more conventional motorcycle, the K100RS, improving still further the original version that broke the ground for BMW in 1983. Since then 35,000 units have been sold and it has been *Motorcycle of the Year* in Germany five years running.

Now the new RS produced 100bhp at 8,000rpm and developed a torque of 100Nm at 6,750rpm, an improvement of 14Nm on its predecessor. In addition the Digital Motor Electronics engine management system, developed for BMW cars, was introduced, giving, BMW claimed, a cleaner and smoother production of power. Visually the changes would not have been easy to detect but another part of the K1 was borrowed to make sure that others knew that this was the latest BMW – the stainless steel exhaust system with the round silencer. Previously the 1,000cc K-series machines used the distinctive square silencer whilst the smaller three cylinder K75 settled for a triangular silencer.

Quite a few parts were used from the K1: the extra-strong front fork, four-piston calliper front brakes (that really were a vast improvement on the older two-piston predecessors), three-spoke light alloy front wheel and the Paralever system as used by the K1 but which started life on the boxer GSs. One thing that remained unchanged was the wind tunnel-developed sports fairing, following the tradition of BMW getting it right from the start when they make a fairing. One other small, but to many significant, change was the option of a lower seat, allowing those with shorter legs to sit comfortably on its 29.92in (760mm) high seat, a saving of 1½in (38mm).

BMW had led the field in anti-lock brake design and it is interesting that, eight years after the first ABS (Anti-Blockier System) brakes were made available to the buying public, very few other manufacturers have made it available and the handful that have limited it to their 'top of the range' models. From 1990 ABS was standard on all of the K-series BMWs. It was not at that stage fitted to the old-style boxers, as there was just not enough electrical output to operate the system. However, the day was not too far off when they would be suitable for boxers too.

ABS is now standard on all but the Funduro.

INCREASED PRODUCTION

By Japanese standards the BMW annual output of some 24,000 motorcycles a year is pretty small beer but BMW have always stressed that they never have been, and never will be, a high volume producer. However, demand was still exceeding supply and in 1990 production was increased by eight percent to 26,000 units a year.

An incredible milestone for the BMW company was reached at the beginning of 1991 when their millionth motorcycle rolled off the production line. Naturally not all of the bikes made started life in Berlin; indeed it was not until 1969 that motorcycle production was centred in the Spandau suburb of Berlin that was previously better known as the prison of war criminal Rudolph Hess. (Prior to that, the majority of bikes were made in Munich with a satellite factory in Eisenach producing the R35 up until 1939. After the war the same bike bearing the EMW logo, which was the same quarters as the BMW badge but using red rather than blue, was produced in what was then East Germany.) The millionth motorcycle was wheeled off the line in front of the assembled press with the finished product going to the German Red Cross. What was astounding about the history of the marque is that, at the time, of the million motorcycles produced half of them were known to be still on the road. That is quite a record, possibly unmatched by any other manufacturer, and a terrific testimony to the reliability and desirability of the marque.

AN RT VERSION OF THE R75

Over the years BMW have developed a pattern of introducing new models; usually the sports version comes first followed by the GS and a road model with, finally, the touring RT. So it was with the K75, but this time it

Bruce Preston (right) and Terry Snelling of Motorcycle News *riding the then new K75C in Norway – or Sweden, or maybe Germany or Spain. The ride from the Arctic Circle to Gibraltar took ten days.*

took some six years before we saw the K75RT. Basically it was the same liquid-cooled three-cylinder engine as had been used by numerous models with modified K100RT fairing. For many riders the touring 750 was the model that they had been waiting for, but sales were not record breaking, possibly because the model had been so long coming, and in 1996 BMW discontinued all the three-cylinder machines. This was a pity, for, to me, it is the most attractive and forgiving of the K-series bikes to ride and provides more than enough power for normal, or even abnormal, use. Another advantage of the 750 was that it fell into a lower insurance category. An interesting option was a three-way catalytic converter.

STILL FAITH IN THE BOXER

At the same time as the K75RT was launched BMW produced up-dated versions of their

popular *Geländestrasse* dual-purpose motor-cycles. They were the first to have the interesting, but rarely understood, Paralever rear suspension. The looks were transformed with a new frame-mounted cockpit fairing incorporating the higher powered headlamp used on the K75S. Now the GS, available in 798 or 980cc form, looked much more like the motorcycles that had earned their spurs in the gruelling Paris–Dakar rally. Indeed, so close was the image, if not the product, that BMW eventually called it the Paris–Dakar.

Perhaps the most interesting innovation of this model was the use of tubeless tyres on a spoked wheel, the first on a production motorcycle. To achieve this the spoke heads were put outside the tyre bead with the threaded spoke end being at the hub rather than, as more usually, at the rim end. Not only was it now possible to use tubeless tyres but spokes could now be replaced without the need to remove the tyre from the rim. The system was very clever and is still being used. A knock-on effect of this allowed a larger

*Style and colour
on the R100GS
Paris–Dakar.*

brake calliper to be used as the wheel was slimmer than before. In consequence, the brakes, by Brembo, were a vast improvement.

Aggressive new colours, Carica Blue, Avus black (not as boring as it sounds!) and Marrakech Red (with the most colourful being Avus black with yellow), all had names that recalled BMW's sporting history. A mini-crash bar surrounded the headlamp and, although the new GS was not really intended for serious off-road work it was more than a poseur's machine, as I found when I asked it to climb the 10,000ft (3,000m) Sani Pass which connects South Africa to Lesotho. With a full complement of luggage and my wife on the back the big 1,000cc motorcycle clawed its way up the rocky road, negotiating the regular boulder strewn hairpins with the surefootedness that showed where it had served its apprenticeship. The 20-mile (32km) climb took well over an hour but the rewards at the top were worth it. Coming down again was something else but by avoiding using the brakes wher-

The highest unmade road in Africa. The Sani Pass proved no obstacle to the R100GS but certainly taxed the rider.

ever possible I completed the adventure without dropping the bike onto its expensive bodywork.

Back in 1981 I owned one of the first BMW R80GSs to be made and to me it was, and still is, the most pleasing BMW I have ever ridden. Unfortunately that pleasure did not extend to the pillion seat and, in spite of attempts to improve things with a new dualseat, it became clear that if I wanted to continue to share my motorcycling with my wife it was not going to be on this motorcycle, for any distance over 100 miles was misery for her. So I sold it, a decision I have regretted ever since. The new version was so changed that hardly anything of the old GS

still remained. I had to admit that the new machine was a better motorcycle in every way but for all that I loved 'my' R80GS with its custom smoke red colour scheme, a one-off produced by BMW for a photo session.

PRODUCTION STILL RISING

Production of BMW motorcycles increased still further. From the 8 per cent increase of 1990 this went to 22.6 per cent in 1992; now 31,589 units were manufactured of which 25,761 were R-series, 11,408 1,000cc Ks and 760s and 750s. This was at a time when

Familiar bridge in Sydney, Australia. The bike is Malcolm Dorroch's K100RT, loaned during a visit to Oz.

world motorcycle sales were dropping significantly: in the ten years prior to 1991 new machine sales had halved.

The R, which by now was supposed to be dead and buried, was still kicking in its grave. Since 1983 nearly 100,000 K100s had been made, quite a number bearing in mind that, between 1923, when the first boxer was made, to the launch of the millionth BMW in 1991, 634,000 units were made, 230,000 of these being singles ranging in size from 200cc to 400cc. Coincidentally, from 1923 to 1939, arguably BMW's heyday when their motorcycles were world beaters, production amounted to 164,000 units, rather less than the number of Ks produced in the eight years from 1983 to 1991. To return to the earlier mention that half of the BMWs made since 1923 were still in use, the breakdown of these figures is interesting. Not surprisingly most

of the models can be found in Germany (144,000) with the USA coming second (68,000), France next with 43,000, then Italy (40,000), Britain (36,000) and Spain (26,000). Perhaps the most surprising figure of all tells us that 21,000 BMWs are still in use in Japan.

MORE GEE-GEES FOR THE BIG K

Rarely a year passes without a new BMW, or at least a different version of the same one, being introduced. There was quite a difference in the big Ks for 1992; capacity was increased to 1,092cc with the arrival of the K1100LT. Theoretically it should have made for a harsher machine, but far from it. I collected a new K1100LT and rode it to the

On the launch of the K1100LT; when it wasn't snowing it was raining, but I was snug in my new BMW Gore-tex suit.

Getting closer to the Honda Gold Wing by the day – the K1100LT.

south of France, crossing the Alps of Haute-Provence and taking in the thrilling Route Napoleon, across the mountains with snow piled high all the way. It rained all the way when it was not snowing, and should have been a miserable journey. It was not, for the arrival of another innovation, the electric windscreen, helped me to get the optimum weather protection and I stayed warm and dry, not only behind the screen but in another BMW product, the Gore-tex riding suit. Expensive, but effective.

BMW were the first to go in for catalytic converters in a big way and the new 1100 had a closed loop cat, the same as the one used on the K1 and K100. These can only work properly with complete electronic management, which the BMW had in the form of Digital Motor Electronics (Motoronic). In consequence, the emission of hydrocarbons was reduced by 77 per cent, with 74 per cent less carbon monoxide and 84 per cent less oxides of nitrogen. It was not possible to use a catalytic converter on the boxer BMW of the time so on this the company settled for the Pulse Air System (PAS), a simpler arrangement that reduces emissions of hydrocarbons by 30 per cent and carbon monoxide by 40 per cent.

A VISION OF THE FUTURE

Like all motorcycle manufacturers, BMW are constantly looking to the future. Perhaps their most ambitious concept was made public in 1992 with the unnamed bike with a roof. Stylish and technically interesting it featured hub-centre steering (very similar to the front steering arrangement on the soon-to-be-introduced Yamaha GTS), car-sized tyres, total protection of the rider in a monocoque construction and stunning good looks. Is this the way of the future? Not yet, but who knows what will happen? Interestingly the Swiss Economobile is made using the same concept and engine but without the BMW's style. An interesting machine though.

BOXERS STILL FIGHTING

In spite of the success of the Ks (or maybe because of it) the flat-twin BMWs were still hanging in. When the K was launched in 1983 BMW were of the view that the days of the boxer were numbered and the new four was the bike of the future. Their customers thought otherwise and, as we will see later,

Definitely a concept bike, shown by BMW as a thought for the future.

Is this the future for BMW? An enclosed three wheeler was BMW's 1992 concept bike.
Is it a car or is it a motorcyle? Will it ever earn the approval of our Eurocrats?

Not a concept bike but the real thing, the Economobile, made in Switzerland.

BMW came back with a new improved boxer that may yet triumph over the water-cooled multis. Meanwhile, BMW had eight boxers in the 1992 catalogue, including a back-to-basics R100R, a simple unadorned roadster that was strong on tradition and weak on weather protection, as indeed it was intended to be. It made me realise how soft I had become sitting behind the windscreen of better protected models. The R100R was to be the last of the traditional boxers for smoke on the horizon told us that a new, very much improved, boxer was not too far away. Meanwhile BMW showed that they were not above a little bit of reaction when they also made a kind of custom version of the R100. Emblazoned with BOXER writ large on the fuel tank and with chromed cylinder heads and various other parts it was . . . interesting. I suppose they sold some but I have never seen one on the road and cannot say that I went to bed dreaming of owning one.

Simple lines.

Not everyone fell about for the syling of the BMW Boxer, designed, maybe, to make some glad to see the back of the old style boxers?

My friend Phyllis O'Brien of Detroit on her new BMW Mystic, just about the last of the old-style boxers to be made.

No monsters in sight as the R1100RS sits alonside Loch Ness.

BMW R259

Or, as it is better known, the new BMW R1100RS.

Tales had long been circulating about the new boxer being developed by BMW. Rumours like this have been around ever since I bought my first BMW nearly forty years ago and whilst they often had substance (I reported back in 1963, in the BMW Journal, that BMW were about to launch a new 900cc motorcycle – I was eleven years early!) rumours alone are not enough: proof was needed. This began to appear in numerous snatched shots of the latest development under test. The pattern was much

the same as when the K-series had been launched a decade earlier. By the time we flew to the Canary Islands to sample the new model its basic design was an open secret.

What we, or at least I, were not ready for was just how good the new engine was. Sitting on the new R1100RS awaiting the off, I just was not prepared for the surge of power that would come my way as I opened the throttle. This was indeed an all-new motorcycle.

Let's start with the engine. Whilst it still had a cylinder sticking out either side there was little else to compare it with the boxer that it was about to replace. For a start the engine housing was not the traditional one

The stylish four-cylinder K1100RS.

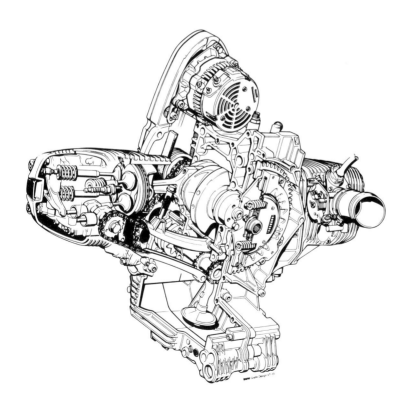

Still faithful to the horizontally opposed twin concept, the new R1100 and R850 engine has lifted that concept onto a different plane.

159

piece as used before but was cast in two almost identical parts. Once again modern science had found a way to achieve, with more reliable casting methods, a simpler but equally efficient result. In this case the oil-sump is a part of both housings.

To allow higher working temperatures the cylinders are cooled by a mixture of air and oil, with oil flowing between the two exhaust valves, making for longer service intervals (now 10,000 kilometres between valve adjustments) and longer life. Four valves are used in each cylinder head; the old central camshaft and long pushrods would have been unsuitable for such an arrangement, so a completely new valve operating system was devised. Now the camshaft is in the cylinder

Monster-type humps on the camels in Lanzarote.

head with chain drive from the crankcase and two short pushrods operate the valves. Amongst the advantages of this is the option of using a smaller drive sprocket and, in consequence, a more slender cylinder head. Even so there is very limited space in the cylinder head. This design is sometimes referred to as of the high-camshaft type.

Although the cylinders still stick out either side they are considerably different from the ones they replace. To allow a large outside surface and thus dissipate the heat more efficiently, the cylinders have cooling fins on the outside specially designed to avoid the hissing noise that such an arrangement usually makes. They are reinforced by connecting pieces that obviate the need for rubber inserts between the cylinders.

Pistons are of the three-ring design (one for oil removal, the other two for compression and sealing). Made in cast alloy the pistons weigh a third less than the old boxer even though they are larger than any produced in the past. Con-rods are made of sintered and forged steel, unlike their predecessors, which were forged but not sintered. This makes for much more accurate production and reliable weight. Now all con-rods weigh the same rather than, as in the past, being sorted into seven weight categories and then machined.

PRODUCTION INNOVATION

Whereas connecting rods are normally cut in half across the boss to enable them to be fitted to the crankshaft, on the R1100 a practice pioneered for BMW cars was used. Here, rather than being cut, the bosses are deliberately fractured, known as cracking, and then joined together again; the joint is almost perfect and just about invisible. Naturally this cracking takes place under controlled conditions. As a result the process is quicker, has lower weight, and allows a better and easier fit. This is the first production motorcycle in the world to use such a system.

The new boxer engine is chock full of innovations. The crankshaft runs on two slide bearings and the lubrication system is controlled by two inter-serrated oil pumps in the front end of the layshaft. Ignition is by Digital Motor Electronics, similar to the arrangement on the K-series and working in the same way; carburettors are now a thing of the past on Spandau-made BMWs for, again as with the K-series, fuel-injection is used, allowing improved performance and economy, better engine response, greater smoothness and refinement, easier maintenance (if you have the right equipment!) and no wear and tear. In addition a three-way

catalytic converter (making lead-free fuel essential) is an option. As on the later boxers, a stainless-steel exhaust system is fitted.

After sixty years BMW had finally completely changed the design of their much loved boxer, although it still looked as a boxer should. There had, of course, been a serious change in 1969 when the cylinders were turned upside down and 12-volt electrics were introduced. Now, though, the cylinders had a distinct tilt. It was not at all the same motorcycle (nor, in fairness, was the R75/5 when it replaced the R60/2) and all the engineering genius that had gone into producing the latest BMW flat-twin had resulted in a motor that knocked spots off the one it would replace. It took me but a few minutes to cry 'the king is dead, long live the king'.

K1100RS.

Nor did the upheaval end there. Even more radical changes had been made to the front end with the introduction of what BMW called their Telelever front suspension system. Simplifying it as much as possible it means that the telescopic front forks are really just oil-filled struts that offer a home for the front wheel. The narrower than normal fork legs are Teflon-coated and contain only oil to allow the sliders an easy passage. The real suspension unit sits behind the front forks and is a central strut measuring just 4.72in (120mm) in length and running perpendicular to the road. It connects the longitudinal control arm with the front section of the motorcycle's frame.

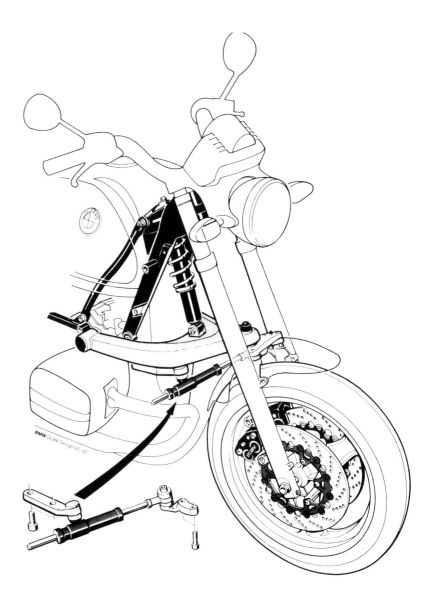

The front forks are really an illusion; it is the small suspension unit behind that does all the work on the new boxer. It works, too.

The secret lies in two maintenance-free ball-joints. The top ball joints runs without any play within the sliding tubes and fork bridge and transmits the steering movement of the telescopic fork. The other ball-joint is bolted to the longitudinal control arm and feeds most of the forces generated when braking to the more stable engine housing. The longitudinal control arm, in turn, is fitted on a swivel mount either side of the engine housing, meaning that the smaller hydraulic unit does all the work and the forks are only required for guiding the motorcycle. BMW have never been considered as being amongst the best-handling of sports motorcycles but now the Paralever/Telelever combination has earned praise even from the marque's critics. The Telelever, particularly, was given top marks by almost all testers, especially as, now, when the rider brakes at night, the headlight does not take a dive. The new system keeps the bike at an even and predictable height.

For the rear suspension the new boxer relies on the now established Paralever rear suspension, as described earlier. Many other features are incorporated on the new R1100RS. Adjustment is offered for not only the seat but also the handlebars and footrests, allowing riders an almost unprecedented choice of riding positions. Twenty years ago BMW became the first manufacturer to offer a wind tunnel-tested fairing that really worked. Even after all of this time the same fairing is still considered amongst the best there is. Now the new boxer has inherited this mantle with a fairing that offers protection and enhanced performance. Few other manufacturers can compete with BMW when it comes to making a fairing that offers the rider protection without limiting performance.

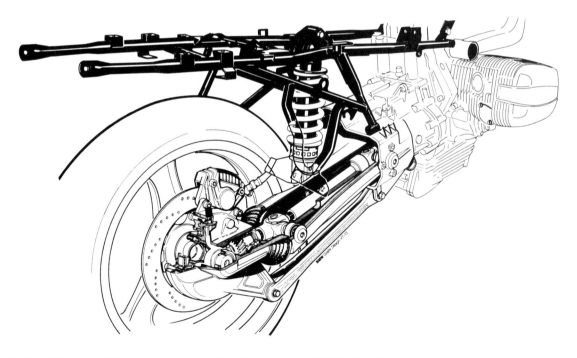

Designed to keep all the suspension working in harmony, BMW's Paralever is rarely fully understood but still appreciated by riders.

MORE THAN JUST BIKES

Around about the time that the new boxers were hitting the headlines BMW entered the activity and leisurewear market even more strongly, offering, in addition to the traditional but rather staid Gore-tex riding suits, a much more colourful range featuring purples, bright red and white suits and lighter 'activity suits'. All, of course, came at a high price. In addition their range was extended to include an active line tent, sleeping bag, sleeping mat and rucksack and even, more recently, a bicycle, all, of course, in matching purples and having that all important badge discreetly but not too well hidden. I chose to try the tent in Ireland, a sure-fire guarantee that it was going to get a baptism of rain if not fire. It did indeed and not a drop of water entered the tent, nor did the sleeping bag fail to keep out the cold.

THE SECOND STAGE – A *GELÄNDESTRASSE* (GS) VERSION

Just a year after the R1100RS was offered to customers we saw the arrival of the R1100GS, a predictable enough move. Using the same basic engine as the RS it did, however, offer a little less power producing 80bhp, some 10bhp less than the RS, making for a noticeably smoother engine. Naturally it followed in the footsteps of the soon to be discontinued R100GS in that it offered all the high-level attributes of that much loved model, of which, combined with the R80GS, 62,000 had been sold. A larger front wheel and high level front mudguard hinted that perhaps the bike would achieve more in bad conditions than most riders would, or even should, expect. It could indeed, for it was derived from motorcycles that had won the Paris–Dakar race on more than one occasion,

once in the hands of a rider who was well under five feet six inches tall so it was no use slightly taller riders like me complaining that the seat was too high! But I did. Stylish and easy to live with I found the softer GS to be even more fun than the RS and thoroughly enjoyed riding it.

By now 1994 was with us and the card of the old boxer was well and truly marked. It was still being made but not for much longer. The traditionalist in me watched its passing, at the end of 1995, with regret but the realist knew that its successor is a much better motorcycle. It had lived, and lived well, for twenty-six years, a fair indication that BMW do not change their motorcycles on whim.

There were just two more pieces in the 1100 jigsaw to be added. Last but one was the unfaired R1100R, a simple, if such a design can ever be considered simple, version that was designed to appeal to the bugs-in-the-teeth people. I thought I was one of them until I rode it a long distance. BMW's excellent fairings have spoiled me and I have come to the conclusion that if I plan to ride far in excess of 60mph (100km/h) I need something to keep wind and weather off me.

THE R1100RT

Had I been able to justify spending nearly £10,000 on a new motorcycle (or, indeed, if I had £10,000 to spend!) I would still have waited for the inevitable RT version to arrive. Just five minutes in the saddle convinced me that I was right. I have ridden every BMW made since 1950 and quite a few made before then. All pale into insignificance when compared with the R1100RT. Based on the R1100RS with the same engine and cycle parts the only real difference is in the fairing. What a difference. Offering sporting looks yet touring protection it has an improvement on BMW's electric windscreen so that the rider can adjust its height and angle by way

For the touring rider the R1100RT is probably the best motorcycle that BMW have ever made, offering sporting looks yet real protection for the rider.

For the author the
most desirable
BMW currently
made, the
R1100RT.

The simple yet
functional cockpit
on the new RT,
featuring fingertip
controls for the
electric windscreen
and ducted warm
air to the rider.

of a handlebar switch (on previous models the switch was in the fairing and not so easy to reach) to all but eliminate not only wind pressure but swirl behind the screen so that the pillion passenger is as protected as the rider. New, non-adjustable, handlebars offer a riding position that suits people like me who prefer to sit upright when riding. In addition to the long-established heated handlebar grips come ducts to allow warm air to be directed from the oil-cooler to the rider to create an ambient temperature some 7° above the norm.

As with all of the new boxers, indeed all BMWs made, luggage equipment is designed to look as though it is part of the motorcycle. Also, in the fairing, is a deep lockable pocket in the left fairing side, ideal for spare gloves and a passport. With a top speed of around 120mph (193kph) it is not fast compared to oriental rockets, but the performance is practical and usable and where there are no speed limits the bike will sit securely at whatever speed the rider chooses, happy in the knowledge that it will not weave or wobble and the rider will be comfortably protected. My kind of bike.

12   A Little Corner of BMW in Italy

So unexpected and surprising was BMW electing to make motorcycles in Italy using Austrian engines that I have looked more deeply at the arrangement than I have at Spandau-made motorcycles. I think it is worth it.

BMW owners over the years have become much more willing to accept change. In fact you could say that they have entered the real world for now we (well, most of us) recognise that change there must be. A quarter of a century ago BMW introduced the /5 series, turning not only the engine but the BMW owner's world upside down. Some of us took years to accept the 'new' boxers as real BMWs and no sooner had we done so than BMW introduced the K-series. It was all too much in the same century and many had to sit in a darkened room with a wet towel over their head. Then, just as they felt able to face the outside world the R1100RS was there to frighten them. What were BMW playing at, as it was only twenty-three years since they last had a major change to the boxers? Is nothing sacred?

All this was, of course, a softening up process for the big one. Judging the die-hards to be still in shock and unable to muster an assault on the ramparts of Spandau they went absolutely over-the-top. All in one go we had chain drive, a single cylinder and, glory be, an engine made in Austria added to a bike assembled in Italy. BMW owners, though, are a canny lot and, world-wide, they bought the new F650 Funduro, as the new model

was called, as fast as they could make them, a ploy designed to fool the company into thinking that they are on the right lines. In another twenty-three years we will all demand boxers and then where will they be?

The only way to cope with such radical thinking is to visit the lion's den and find out just what the hidden agenda is. Maybe, I thought, the 650 was just the prototype of the new boxer with one of the new engines ultimately scheduled to be made poking out either side? Obviously the chain drive is just a temporary measure until they can find a way of making a shaft lighter and cheaper than the chain.

Noale is less than half an hour from Venice, with the Alps towering in the background and is not at all a bad place to work in. As is well documented, the new BMW, although totally under the control of BMW, is assembled at the Aprilia factory using an engine built by Rotax but designed by BMW, taking Rotax's established 650 motor as a basis. My plan was to see how BMW can square their desire for quality with having the motorcycle built by someone else. Easy, really. They have one man, Ewe Becker, *Qualitätsfachingenieur*, responsible for the whole operation. He is a BMW-employed Berliner who, although quite young, is steeped in the tradition of quality and class that has long been the hallmark of BMW. All the rest of the F650 staff are employed by Aprilia and wear company overalls but they are dedicated to the BMW production line.

There are twenty-seven (out of a total of 500 in the works) of them in total and the continuous line occupies one sector of what is a modest-sized factory.

All parts used on motorcycles in this operation are bought in, nothing is made in house, so BMW do not have any trouble ensuring that everything fitted to the F650 is exactly as they want. Just in case, every part arriving in the factory is inspected to ensure that no doubtful ones slip through. It is the first of a number of quality checks. Aprilia also make a single-cylinder 650, the Pegaso, and cynics can be forgiven for thinking that the Funduro is just some clever badge engineering. This is far from being the case as only 2 per cent of the parts used in the Funduro are common to the Pegaso. Maybe the basic dimensions are the same but little else. Back in Austria the engine is very different from its cousin and has four valves (the Pegaso has five) an arrangement that, combined with softer internal cams, makes the Funduro more user-friendly. Before leaving Austria each engine is run for ten minutes and then despatched to Noale dry (i.e. without oil in the crankcase) to reduce the risk of accidents.

There is no comparison between the frames, either, as the Funduros are made by MT of northern Italy and are totally different. Upon arrival, the frames, which are oil-carrying, are thoroughly washed out to reduce the risk of contamination and then passed to the production line, where the real motorcycle is made. First the pre-assembled front wheel and forks (like the rear suspension by Japanese manufacturer Showa) are secured to the frame, giving a nose-down rolling chassis, which is then bolted to a jig ready for its almost three-hour long journey to completion. There are twenty-two stations on the line, each demanding roughly eight minutes. First the engine and rear suspension and then all other underbody parts are fitted to BMW specification.

F650 Funduro in the south of France.

One problem with a rotating production line is that if the operative cannot complete his task in time it might be allowed to pass on, not quite right. On this line each worker has a cord he can pull to stop the line if, for example, things don't fit properly. Help is at hand if need be. Ewe explained that it is so much easier to put things right at the time than later, so no stigma is attached to anyone who asks for help. Most of the staff, compared to those at Spandau, are quite young, with a few having worked for Laverda, who were not too far away before their demise (Laverda are, happily, now back in business but not at Breganze).

When all the cycle parts are in place, another quality control station is introduced. This is before the fuel tank and bodywork are attached, enabling the checker to see more easily if there are any faults. Once satisfied that all is in order the fuel tank and side panels, also made locally, are added to the bike. The tank comes with the tap in place but the badge and filler ring are added at this stage. Now that it is possible to use plastic for fuel tanks, much more interesting things can be done with them and the shape of the F650 tank bears no relation to the one used on the Aprilia. Once assembly is complete and oil and coolant added the bike is pushed to the rolling road, again a dedicated one with rollers for front and rear wheel. Alongside are two Aprilia rolling roads with just a rear wheel roller. Here the engine is started and everything possible checked. If the tester is happy that everything is as it should be he passes the bike to despatch; if he is not satisfied, it is sent to casualty for any defect to be put right. Very few are sent this way.

A final quality check occurs each day when one of the fifty-eight bikes made is selected at random for a major quality check. A list of 400 checks is carried out, including a long road test by the one dedicated quality tester, and to be acceptable the machine has to amass no more than 100 points, some of which are awarded for every fault found. By fault, I mean for example, an almost imperceptible scratch on the silencer, which earned twenty-four points, and an even harder to see fault in the moulding of the plastic side cover, which earned twenty-two. These were the only faults found with the bike being tested the day that I was there. Ewe proudly explained to me that the F650 had been within limits every day since the production line opened less than two years ago and he was quite sure that the level of quality was as high as that of BMW's Spandau motorcycle factory. Incidentally, this points test is applied to every BMW production facility in the world, car or bike. So successful has it been that Aprilia have also introduced the system, but Ewe explained, quietly so as not to offend Roberta, the Aprilia PR lady who was with us, that good as the quality of the Aprilia product was, BMW's was better. Perhaps 'more demanding' is a better description.

I would not have risked my light-hearted introduction to this story had I come away from Noale disappointed in the end product. On the contrary, I was very impressed, for the combination of Italian flair and innovation and BMW precision has resulted in a very attractive motorcycle. Both Aprilia and BMW are comfortable with the partnership and each has added to the other's knowledge and ability. The Italians have shown themselves to be particularly good at finding short cuts without sacrificing quality whilst BMW have demonstrated to Aprilia the importance of serious quality control on production systems. These have been happily embraced by those putting the new F650 together and although they are wearing overalls with Aprilia emblazoned on the back they are now thinking like BMW people. The end result is there for all to see.

Production at Noale is now running at something in the region of 11,000 F650s a year, maybe 10 per cent of the factory's total output. It has been a tremendous success story, with every bike made being sold (the UK's quota last year was 650 machines). More bikes could be made, if more staff were hired, but the hold-up is the difficulty of obtaining enough supplies from outside. For example, only sixty fuel tanks a day can be made on existing moulds so others would need to be created for more tanks. It is an expensive operation that needs serious thought. Given time, BMW will undoubtedly increase their production facility, but not at the expense of quality. Meanwhile enjoy the F650 Funduro. It might not look like a BMW but it is made like one and it is making friends wherever it goes.

NOT QUITE THE COMPLETE JIGSAW

Although, for the forseeable future, the R1100 picture is complete there is another smaller picture emerging. This comes in the shape of the smaller R850, a little brother to the 1100 offering all the virtues of the unfaired R1100 with the slight loss of performance being offset by a sweeter, smoother engine. In all other respects the 850 has the same engine and cycle parts as the 1100 but a lower price tag. Potentially it could be the best new boxer yet made and I think we can look forward to the arrival of maybe a GS and RT version. Watch this space.

A PIECE OF THE JIGSAW GOES MISSING

Sadly, at the same time as the old boxer was being phased out BMW announced that the three-cylinder K75 was also to be dropped. Personally I think that this is a great pity for in many respects the three was a much more pleasing motorcycle to ride than the four. BMW, however, would point to the sales figures and say that the fours always outsold the threes, which cost almost as much to make as the four but by definition had to sell for less. I'll be sad to see the K75 die.

Useful Addresses

BMW Club (Great Britain); any British BMW motorcycle dealer will have an up-to-date address or alternatively it can be obtained from:

The British Motorcyclists Federation
129 Seaforth Avenue
Motspur Park
New Malden
Surrey KT3 6JU.

Isetta Owners Club
The Spinney
Fairmile
Henley-on-Thames
Oxfordshire RG9 6AE.

Specifications for all BMW models since 1923

Model	Year	Capacity (cc)	Number of cylinders	Bore-stroke (mm)	Power (PS/rpm)	Valve operation	Gears	Weight
R32	1923	486	twin	68×68	8.5 @ 3,300	SV	3	245lb (120Kg)
		(494 from 1925)						
R39	1925	247	single	68×68	6.5 @ 4,400	OHV	3	242.5lb (110Kg)
R37	1925	494	twin	68×68	16 @ 4,000	OHV	3	295lb (134Kg)
R42	1926	494	twin	68×68	12 @ 4,000	SV	3	278lb (126Kg)
R47	1927	494	twin	68×68	18 @ 4,000	OHV	3	287lb (130Kg)
R52	1928	487	twin	78×63	12 @ 3,400	SV	3	335lb (152Kg)
R57	1928	492	twin	68×68	18 @ 4,000	OHV	3	331lb (150Kg)
R62	1928	745	twin	78×78	18 @ 3,400	SV	3	342lb (155Kg)
R63	1928	734	twin	83×68	24 @ 4,000	OHV	3	342lb (155Kg)
R11	1929	740	twin	78×78	18 @ 3,400	SV	3	357lb (162Kg)
R16	1929	730	twin	83×68	25 @ 4,000	OHV	3	364lb (165Kg)
R2	1931	198	single	63×64	6 @ 3,500	OHV	3	242.5lb (110Kg)
R4	1932	398	single	78×84	12 @ 3,500	OHV	3	302lb (137Kg)
					(4 speed from1933)			
R12	1935	745	twin	78×78	18 or 20 @ 3,400	SV	4	408lb (185Kg)
R17	1935	736	twin	83×68	33 @ 5,500	OHV	4	403.5lb (183Kg)
R3	1936	305	single	68×84	11 @ 4,200	OHV	4	328.5lb (149Kg)
R5	1936	494	twin	68×68	24 @ 5,800	OHV	4	364lb (165Kg)
R20	1937	192	single	60×68	8 @ 5,400	OHV	3	287lb (130Kg)
R35	1937	340	single	72×84	14 @ 4,500	OHV	4	342lb (155Kg)
R6	1937	596	twin	70×78	18 @ 4,800	SV	4	386lb (175Kg)
R23	1938	247	single	68×68	10 @ 5,400	OHV	3	298lb (135Kg)
R51	1938	494	twin	68×68	24 @ 5,600	OHV	4	401lb (182Kg)
R61	1938	596	twin	70×78	18 @ 4,800	SV	4	406lb (184Kg)
R66	1938	597	twin	69.8×78	30 @ 5,300	OHV	4	412lb (187Kg)
R71	1938	745	twin	78×78	22 @ 4,600	SV	4	412lb (187Kg)
R75	1941	745	twin	78×78	26 @ 4,000	OHV	4+ reverse×2	926lb (420Kg)

(This was only available for the military and came as a complete sidecar outfit with sidecar drive and reverse gears)

Model	Year	Capacity (cc)	Number of cylinders	Bore-stroke (mm)	Power (PS/rpm)	Valve operation	Gears	Weight
R24	1949	247	single	68×68	12 @ 5,600	OHV	4	287lb (130Kg)
R25	1950	245	single	68×68	12 @ 5,600	OHV	4	309lb (140Kg)
R51/2	1950	494	twin	68×68	24 @ 5,800	OHV	4	408lb (185Kg)
R51/3	1951	490	twin	68×68	24 @ 5,800	OHV	4	419lb (190Kg)
R67	1951	590	twin	72×73	6 @ 5,500	OHV	4	423lb (192Kg)
R68	1952	590	twin	72×73	35 @ 7,000	OHV	4	425.5lb (193Kg)
R25/3	1953	245	single	68×68	13 @ 5,800	OHV	4	331lb (150Kg)
R26	1955	245	single	68×68	15 @ 6,400	OHV	4	348lb (158Kg)
R50	1955	490	twin	68×68	26 @ 5,800	OHV	4	430lb (195Kg)
R69	1955	590	twin	72×73	35 @ 6,800	OHV	4	445lb (202Kg)
R60	1956	590	twin	72×73	28 @ 5,600	OHV	4	430lb (195Kg)
			(US version with telescopic front-forks introduced in 1967)					
R27	1960	245	single	68×68	18 @ 7,400	OHV	4	357lb (162Kg)
R50S	1960	490	twin	68×68	35 @ 7,650	OHV	4	436.5lb (198Kg)

Model	Year	Capacity (cc)	Number of cylinders	Bore-stroke (mm)	Power (PS/rpm)	Valve operation	Gears	Weight
R69S	1960	590	twin	72×73	42 @ 7,000	OHV	4	445lb (202Kg)
(US version with telescopic front-forks introduced in 1967)								
R50/5	1969	494	twin	67×70.6	32 @ 6,400	OHV	4	408lb (185Kg)
R60/5	1969	599	twin	73.5×70.6	40 @ 6,400	OHV	4	419lb (190Kg)
R75/5	1969	745	twin	82×70.6	50 @ 6,500	OHV	4	419lb (190Kg)
R60/6	1973	599	twin	73×70.6	40 @ 6,500	OHV	5	441lb (200Kg)
R75/6	1973	745	twin	82×70.6	50 @ 6,500	OHV	5	441lb (200Kg)
R90/6	1973	898	twin	90×70.6	60 @ 6,500	OHV	5	441lb (200Kg)
R90S	1973	898	twin	90×70.6	67 @ 7,000	OHV	5	452lb (205Kg)
R60/7	1976	599	twin	73.5×70.6	40 @ 6,400	OHV	5	430lb (195Kg)
R75/7	1976	745	twin	82×70.6	50 @ 6,200	OHV	5	430lb (195Kg)
R100/7	1976	980	twin	94×70.6	60 @ 6,500	OHV	5	430lb (195Kg)
R100S	1976	980	twin	94×70.6	65 @ 6,600	OHV	5	441lb (200Kg)
					(70 @ 7,250 from 1978)			
R100RS	1976	980	twin	94×70.6	70 @ 7,250	OHV	5	463lb (210Kg)
(Re-launched with monoshock rear-suspension and 60PS engine in 1986)								
R80/7	1977	785	twin	84.8×70.6	55 @ 7,000	OHV	5	430lb (195Kg)
(50PS @ 7,250 lower-powered version also made)								
R100RT	1978	980	twin	94×70.6	70 @ 7,250	OHV	5	516lb (234Kg)
(Re-launched with monoshock rear-suspension and 60PS engine in 1987)								
R45	1978	473	twin	70×61.5	35 @ 7,250	OHV	5	452lb (205Kg)
(27PS @ 6,500 lower-powered version also made)								
R65	1978	650	twin	82×61.5	45 @ 7,250	OHV	5	452lb (205Kg)
(Re-launched with monoshock rear-suspension and 48PS engine in 1984)								
R100T	1978	980	twin	94×70.6	70 @ 7,250	OHV	5	436.5lb (198Kg)
(65PS @ 6,600 lower-powered version also made)								
R65LS	1983	650	twin	82×61.5	50 @ 7,250	OHV	5	408lb (185Kg)
R100	1983	980	twin	94×70.6	70 @ 7,000	OHV	5	436.5lb (198Kg)
R100CS	1983	980	twin	94×70.6	70 @ 7,000	OHV	5	441lb (200Kg)
R80GS	1980	797.5	twin	84.8×70.6	50 @ 6,500	OHV	5	368lb (167Kg)
R80ST	1982	797.5	twin	84.8×70.6	50 @ 6.500	OHV	5	403.5lb (183Kg)
R80RT	1982	797.5	twin	84.8×70.6	50 @ 6,500	OHV	5	472lb (214Kg)
(Re-launched with monoshock rear-suspension in 1984)								
R80	1984	797.7	twin	84×70.6	50 @ 6,500	OHV	5	463lb (210Kg)
R80G/S	1988	797.7	twin	84×70.6	50 @ 6,500	OHV	5	421lb (191Kg)
(A Paris–Dakar version was also made with a larger fuel tank)								
R100G/S	1988	980	twin	94×70.6	60 @ 6,500	OHV	5	463lb (210Kg)
K100	1983	987	four	67×70	90 @ 8,000	OHC	5	527lb (239Kg)
K100RS	1984	987	four	67×70	90 @ 8,000	OHC	5	558lb (253Kg)
K100RT	1984	987	four	67×70	90 @ 8,000	OHC	5	580lb (263Kg)
K75C	1985	740	three	67×70	75 @ 8,500	OHC	5	503lb (228Kg)
K75S	1986	740	three	67×70	75 @ 8,500	OHC	5	518lb (235Kg)
K100LT	1987	987	four	67×70	90 @ 8,000	OHC	5	580lb (263Kg)
K1	1989	987	four	67×70	100 @ 8,000	OHC	5	569lb (258Kg)
K100RS (4 valve)	1990	987	four	67×70	100 @ 8,000	OHC	5	570lb (259Kg)
R100GS (Paris–Dakar)	1990	980	twin	94×70.6	60 @ 6,500	OHV	5	515lb (234Kg)
K1100LT	1992	1092	four	70.5×70	100 @ 7,500	OHC	5	639lb (290Kg)
R100R	1992	980	twin	94×70.6	60 @ 6,500	OHV	5	480lb (218Kg)

Model	Year	Capacity (cc)	Number of cylinders	Bore-stroke (mm)	Power (PS/rpm)	Valve operation	Gears	Weight	
K1100RS	1993	1092	four	70.5×70	100 @ 7,500	OHC	5	639lb	(290Kg)
R1100RS	1993	1085	twin	99×70.5	90 @ 7,250	HC	5	535lb	(243Kg)
R80R	1993	798	twin	84.8×70.6	50 @ 6,500	OHV	5	478lb	(217Kg)
R1100GS	1994	1085	twin	99×90.75	80 @ 6,750	HC	5	535lb	(243Kg)
F650	1994	652	single	100×83	48 @ 6,500	OHC	5	416lb	(189Kg)
R850R	1994	848	twin	87.5×70.5	70 @ 7,000	HC	5	518lb	(235Kg)
R1100R	1994	1085	twin	99×70.5	80 @ 6,750	HC	5	518lb	(235Kg)
R100 Mystik	1994	980	twin	94×70.6	60 @ 6,500	OHV	5	480lb	(218kg)
R110RT	1995	1085	twin	99×70.5	90 @ 7,250	HC	5	621lb	(282Kg)

Note: SV = side valve
  OHV = overhead valve
  OHC = overhead camshaft

Index